TOTAL QUALITY COUNSELING

A COMPREHENSIVE MANUAL
FOR
ELEMENTARY/MIDDLE SCHOOL COUNSELORS

WRITTEN BY
DAVID BURGESS

TOTAL QUALITY COUNSELING

10-DIGIT ISBN: 1-884063-44-6
13-DIGIT ISBN: 978-1-884063-44-2

Revised/Reprinted 1995/2001/2009

Published by mar*co products, inc.
1443 Old York Road
Warminster, PA 18974
1-800-448-2197
www.marcoproducts.com

Photographs provided by www.shutterstock.com

PRINTED IN THE U.S.A.

TABLE OF CONTENTS

A MESSAGE FROM THE AUTHOR

My goal in creating this manual was to produce a truly practical aid for the busy counselor—brand new or experienced, or the future counselor enrolled in a master's degree program. Rather than take a textbook style approach, I decided to use an easy-to-access question and answer format, and provide easily adaptable forms. I drew upon my 10 years of experience as a school counselor and several years as a state consultant in school counseling as the basis for the book and for the many opinions expressed herein.

At about the same time I conceived the idea for this practical manual, I became involved in something called Total Quality Management or TQM. My initial involvement was through my position as a commissioned officer in the U.S. Coast Guard Reserve. I was trained to be a quality facilitator and was given the task of training others as well as applying the concepts of TQM to real world problems. At the Virginia Department of Education, I also became involved in TQM within educational settings as the department entered into an exciting partnership with the Xerox Corporation to share its award winning strategies with school districts in Virginia.

Since the publication of *Total Quality Counseling* in 1991, I have coauthored/ edited a book published by the American School Counselor Association entitled *Quality Leadership and the Professional School Counselor*. For that book, my writing partner (Rebecca Dedmond) and I created a model for applying the principles of TQM into school settings and provided practical strategies for school counselors to demonstrate leadership in school reform and in making schools truly customer focused—that is to say, student focused. In the back of my mind for both books have been two fundamental concepts:

1. Communication skills are leadership skills; school counselors alone in the school are extensively trained in human communication skills and systematic problem-solving with individuals and groups.

2. School counselors can best demonstrate leadership in school reform by providing comprehensive, developmental school counseling programs.

Since this book was first written in 1991, and revised in 1995, 2001, and 2008 the world of education and the school counselor's many roles continue to change and evolve. For this latest revision, I am indebted to Ms. Lauren Savage, a school counselor at my school, for assisting me in updating this edition. Specifically, she revised the *Behavior Contract*, included a new *Teacher Referral Form, Initial Interview Form*, and *Umbrella* and *Shield Activities*. She also included a core content session on anger management for the *Communication Group Model* in Chapter 4, scenarios for "You" and "I" messages, testing tips, and a form applicable to the *Talk It Out* procedure. New to this edition as well is a form for student self-referrals from classrooms, and an intake form called *Speak Out* for students new to your school.

I am most grateful to the more than 6,000 professionals who have purchased my book and always welcome comments (pro and con). Please send your comments to me in care of Mar*co Products, and let me know how you have added your own unique talents and ideas to those in the book.

CHAPTER 1
DEVELOPMENTAL ELEMENTARY/ MIDDLE SCHOOL COUNSELING

What skills will today's children need in the world of tomorrow?

Today's children will need:

- Basic skills (reading, math, writing, etc.).
- Interpersonal skills (ability to get along with others).
- Communication skills (oral as well as written).

What is a developmental approach to a school counseling program?

A developmental approach helps students as they develop:

- Physically.
- Emotionally.
- Socially.
- Cognitively.

What are the goals of a developmental school counseling program?

As stated by Myrick in *Developmental Guidance and Counseling: A Practical Approach* (1993), the goals of a developmental school counseling program are:

- Understanding the school environment.
- Understanding self and others.
- Understanding attitudes and behavior.
- Developing decision-making and problem-solving skills.
- Developing interpersonal and communication skills.
- Developing school-success skills.
- Creating career awareness and educational planning.
- Creating community pride and involvement.

What are some things a comprehensive developmental elementary school counseling program is not?

A comprehensive developmental elementary school counseling program Is not:

- Crisis-driven.
- Helping students feel good for feeling-good's sake.
- Only for students with problems.

What does research show are the benefits of a developmental elementary school counseling program?

Research shows improvement in:

- School attitudes and work habits, which correlate to dropping out or staying in school.
- Peer relationships and communication skills, which correlate to vital skills and understandings employers want in their workers.
- Motivation, behavior, and grades, which correlate to learning and achievement (basic academic skills).

What are the implications of a developmental approach for you as a school counselor?

Counselors know that social and emotional development (or lack of it) can positively or negatively affect learning. A developmental approach gives counselors the opportunity to promote positive growth in this area. (See pages 107-108, for a chart of developmental ages and program implications for counselors.)

Why are school counselors needed in all schools?

Counselors are needed:

- To help all students learn (achieve) as efficiently and effectively as possible.
- To have an impact on the major skill areas that are necessary for success as an adult.

How do you, the counselor, reach all students in your school?

Students in the school are reached through:

- Prevention services.
- Intervention services.
- Developmentally-sound practices.

What is the target of prevention and intervention services?

The target of prevention and intervention services is improved self-esteem which is shown by responsible behavior and academic achievement.

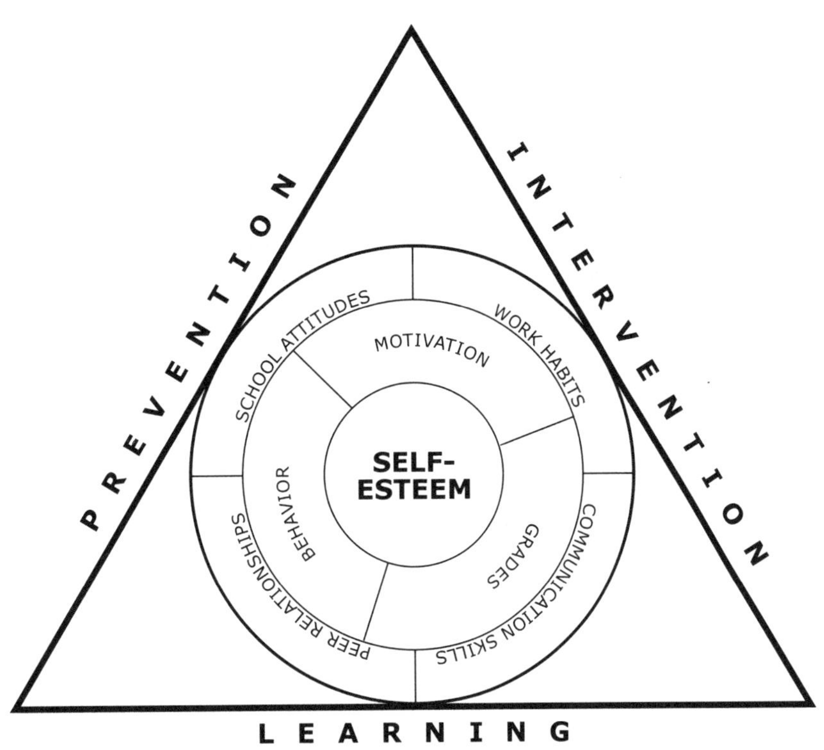

▶ **Why is improving self-esteem the target of prevention and intervention services?**

Self-esteem is positively correlated to achievement.

▶ **Self-esteem and self-concept seem to be used interchangeably. Are they the same?**

No.

▶ **What is self-esteem?**

Self-esteem is:

- Self-respect.
- A gauge of the level of confidence one has in one's ability to solve problems.
- Positively related to learning.

▶ **What is self-concept?**

Self-concept is:

- The basic picture people carry in their heads about their ability to be successful or unsuccessful as they are faced with new tasks in their lives.
- Relatively stable.
- Difficult to change.

▶ **Can we see, taste, feel, hear, or smell self-esteem?**

No.

▶ **How do we know when someone has or does not have healthy self-esteem?**

We see the behavioral results:

HEALTHY SELF-ESTEEM	POOR SELF-ESTEEM
Responsible behavior	Irresponsible behavior
Goal-directed behavior	Academic underachievement
Achievement	Failure

▶ **How are self-concept and self-esteem related?**

Think of a camera analogy. If you help students raise their self-esteem, you help to give their self-concept picture a clearer focus (away from a negative, blurry focus to a clearer, more positive focus).

How does raising self-esteem help students have a more positive focus?

This happens because:

- Clearer thinking and belief in one's ability to cope leads to small successes.
- Small successes in dealing with problems give students something positive to build on—to believe they can affect their environment.
- Small successes today can lead to bigger successes tomorrow.
- Students can not build on failure, only on success.

What is your goal for each student in your school?

The goal is to help each student learn as much as possible.

How can your overriding goal be to help students learn? Isn't that a classroom teacher's task?

Your position as a counselor is instructional support. This means you coordinate with teachers to address that which interferes with learning.

Are counselors therapists?

No. Counselors:

- Are not trained therapists.
- Do not have time for in-depth therapy even if they are so qualified.
- Cannot directly affect the circumstances of students' home lives.
- Do not directly give students the academic skills necessary to be a future worker.
- Are behavior change experts!

How can you help each student learn?

The chart below shows the allocation of the counselor's time in a balanced developmental approach.

COORDINATION (20%)	
Prevention (40%)	**Intervention (40%)**
Developmental small-group counseling Classroom guidance Career-education projects Peer-helper program/projects	Individual counseling Small-group counseling (problem-centered) Consultation with: Child Study Team—Community agencies Parents—Teachers—Principal

Are guidance and counseling the same?

No. They are often mistakenly used interchangeably to the detriment of both concepts.

What is guidance?

Guidance is a program of services you provide to students, parents, teachers, administrators, and community members.

- These services are both direct and indirect as shown in the chart below.

INDIRECT (SUPPORT STUDENT LEARNING)	DIRECT (TO STUDENT)
Consulting Career-education projects Peer-helper programs Coordinating functions	Counseling Classroom guidance Group guidance

- Therefore counseling is but one of the services provided in a comprehensive program of guidance services.

What is a balanced guidance program?

A balanced guidance program is a 100% program with no add-ons.

A balanced guidance program can become unbalanced if you are asked to coordinate non-guidance functions.

A sample of a balanced guidance program can be found on page 152.

What is the number one factor that will determine a counselor's success?

It is not:

- Your skills.
- Your personality.
- Your attitude.
- Your appearance.

Then what is it? It is:

- Your image.
- What you do and do not do as perceived by your "customers."

▶ Who are your "customers"?

Your "customers" are those who receive guidance services such as:

- Students.
- Teachers.
- Parents.
- Administrators.
- School board members.
- Community agency personnel.
- Medical personnel.

Each of your "customers" has a perception of what you do and how well you do it.

▶ What affects your "customer's" perception of what you do?

Your "customer's" perception of your role is affected by:

- Facts.
- Opinions.
- Hearsay.
- Prejudgment.
- Past contact with school counselors.

▶ Is this perceptual image process fair?

No, but it is a fact of life.

▶ What image do you want?

You want to be viewed as a:

- Person who can make a difference.
- Pro-active change agent.
- Non-judgmental listener who cares.

▶ What image don't you want?

You do not want to be viewed as a:

- Paper pusher/quasi-administrator.
- Smoother-overer who makes excuses for incomplete tasks.
- Disciplinarian.

▶ How can you foster a pro-active image?

This can be done if you:

- Become an integral part of your school.
- Interact in large or small ways with everyone on your faculty, as well as PTA/PTO members.
- Act rather than react in large and small ways to the responsibilities of the job.

▶ Can you solve students' problems for them?

No. If you "buy-in" to the idea you can wave a magic wand and "fix" problems, you are doomed to fail and will burn out.

▶ But if you can't solve students' problems, how will your "customers" know when you've been successful?

Your primary "customers," the students, will know when they:

- Improve academically and behaviorally as you have stressed improvement over and over.
- Have more self-confidence because you have been a positive reinforcer.
- Are able to accept their mistakes and learn from them because you have treated mistakes as something to learn from, not something to be punished for.

Put another way, your goal as a counselor is to help your students to:

- Think for themselves.
- Believe in themselves.
- Help themselves.
- Make lemonade from life's lemons.

▶ What is Total Quality Management or TQM?

TQM is a set of principles based on a philosophy. The "father" of TQM was a man named W. Edwards Deming (see his seminal work *Out of the Crisis 1986* for more information). It was Deming and his ideas which helped turn Japan into a world leader in quality manufacturing. In fact, the highest quality award in Japan is named for this American—the Deming Award. The philosophy underlying TQM is called continuous improvement of processes.

All work done in any organization is the result of human beings performing tasks within work processes. For example, think of all the processes involved in educating a child from the first day of school until the end of the year. The teacher supplies instruction to the student, receives support from the principal, supplies input to the parent(s) of the student, etc. Continuous improvement of processes is the vehicle for achieving "quality" and forever improving services to students.

But who determines what quality is? In education, is it the teacher? the principal? the parent? No, it is the student who is the "customer" as well as the product of the learning process.

Therefore, at its most basic, TQM is meeting the needs of the "customer" through continuous improvement of work processes. In schools, TQM is shown by a student-focused curriculum in which students demonstrate mastery of both academic content and process skills, such as thinking, collaborating, communicating, problem-solving, etc. In addition, it is shown by students developing positive attitudes toward learning and themselves.

Quality organizations have other attributes in addition to strong "customer" focus and continuous improvement of processes, such as:

- Self-managed teams (based on the fact that human beings are intrinsically, not extrinsically, motivated to succeed as all counselors know).
- Measurement and monitoring of work processes (not just results).
- Belief that total involvement in, and responsibility for, quality rests with all employees.
- Systematic support for quality from all divisions/areas of the organization.

Quality organizations employ the "voice of the customer" into all planning and organizational actions. No matter how good they might be, they strive to continuously improve work processes. If the "customer" is not satisfied, the organization has not succeeded.

How is TQM related to a developmental school counseling program?

School counselors have the unique training and experience to compliment the academic preparation of students. Counselors are communication experts, and communication skills are leadership skills in today's workplace.

Because of the emphasis on working in teams, persons in TQM organizations must be able to get along with others, solve problems in group situations, arrive at a group consensus in decision making, and monitor their own work processes. No matter how technically advanced the workplace becomes, these "people" skills will remain important.

A developmental school counseling program can address the vital process skills students must have in the workplace of tomorrow, as well as intervene in problems that interfere with learning today.

Summary:

Elementary school guidance and counseling aims to impact students' self-esteem through intervention and prevention services. Students develop socially and emotionally as well as physically and cognitively.

The counselor's image as a caring, non-judgmental adult who helps students, teachers, and parents learn from mistakes is crucial. The counselor's job is a multifaceted one of influencing positive behavior change in students and the important adults in students' lives.

A comprehensive developmental elementary school counseling program is a 100% program, balanced between prevention and intervention.

Counselors possess communication skills which are leadership skills.

Key Processes Of The School Counseling Program

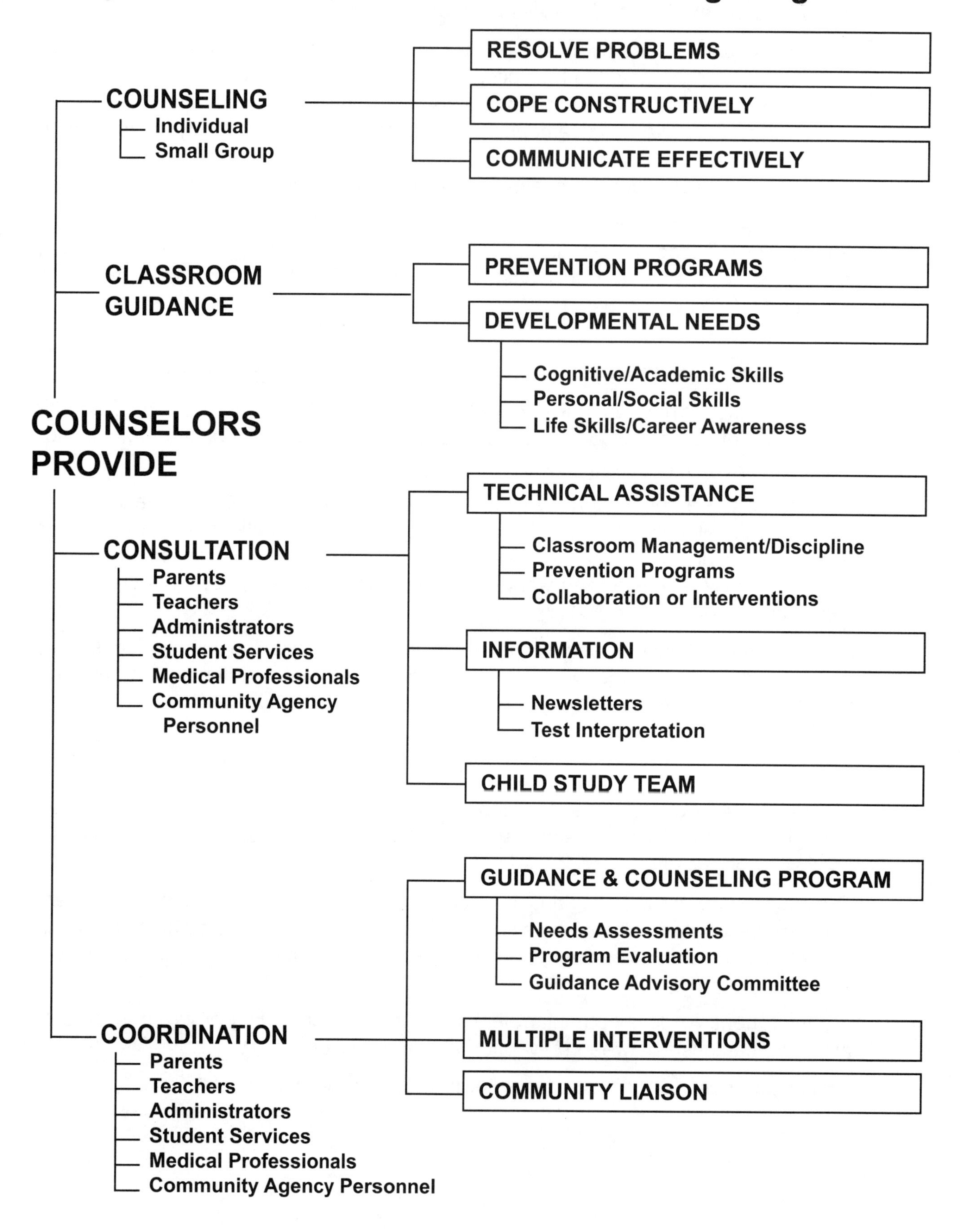

CHAPTER 2
COUNSELING SKILLS

What is your role as a counselor?

Your role is:

- To teach students that choices have consequences.
- To help students develop self-discipline.
- Not to administer punishment or discipline.

What is your role in helping students learn?

Your role is to help children and adults learn from their mistakes.

- Learning from one's mistakes, so they aren't repeated, is called "experience."

What skills will you need?

A skilled counselor can:

- Listen in a non-judgmental manner.
- Question in a non-threatening way.
- Make restatements for clarification.
- Use feeling statements such as "You" messages and "I" messages to establish trust.

Why is the ability to communicate so essential?

It allows for a better understanding of self and others.

Through a process of self-disclosure and feedback, a trust relationship can be developed, feelings and actions explored, alternative courses of action considered, and the student's own plan of action developed to change his/her behavior. You can't change a student's behavior. They must do it themselves.

What is so difficult about listening?

Non-judgmental listening means accepting the person and what has been done even though you don't necessarily agree with the person's behavior or ideas.

Listening invokes the use of more than just one's ears.

- The ears are used for hearing words and ideas. They help you to know what is said and what is not said.
- The eyes are used to observe body language or nonverbal behavior. They are also used to establish eye contact.
- The torso is used to lean in toward a person, giving him/her your full attention.
- The mouth allows you to say things to show that you hear and that you care about what is said.
- The mind helps you to perceive the feelings—positive, negative, or both—behind the words.

▶ What are the two types of questions?

Open questions invite sharing and explanation of information.

- Who?
  - "Who went with you?"
- What?
  - "What do you think about him?"
- Where?
  - "Where did you go?"
- When?
  - "When will you go?"
- How?
  - "How will you handle it?"

Closed questions encourage short answers and can block communication.

- Closed questioning can be, in reality, a stating of the questioner's opinions.
- It can also be the type of questioning that requires a "Yes" or "No" answer or other one-word answers.
- Examples of closed questions are:
  - "You don't like him, do you?"
  - "Did you go there with him?"
  - "Did you go home or to school?"
  - "Will you go today, tomorrow, or next week?"
  - "Will you fix it or throw it away?"

▶ Why not ask a question that begins with the word "why?"

"Why" questions put people on the defensive.

They engender defensiveness and excuse-making.

People, in general, and especially children, often don't really know why they do what they do.

"Why" questions can also be interpreted as your opinion. For example:

- "Why don't you study more often?" implies you should study more often.

▶ What if you, as the counselor, need to find out "Why" or "Why not?"

Change the "why" question to a "how" or a "what" question.

- Instead of, "Why did you hit him?" say, "What made you want to hit him?"
- Instead of, "Why don't you like school?" say, "How could school be a better place for you?"
- Instead of "Why don't you study more?" say, "What keeps you from studying?"
- Or you can always use "Can you tell me more about what happened?"

What is the purpose of restatements?

Restatements can clarify factual details you have heard, such as:

- "You went home, ate dinner, started to study, and fell asleep."

Restatements can also be a summary of the main idea(s) you are hearing, such as:

- "Tom, you seem to be saying that you like school, but dislike English class."

What are feeling statements?

Feeling statements:

- Show empathy for the feelings you hear behind what is said and not said.
- Help build a relationship because the student perceives you care and are trying to understand him/her.
- Facilitate self-disclosure. The message you send is that you are listening, you care, and you are not judging.

What is the key element in a feeling statement?

A feeling statement must use either a positive or negative feeling word.

POSITIVE FEELING WORDS	NEGATIVE FEELING WORDS
approved	afraid
brave	angry
cheerful	annoyed
competent	blamed
delighted	betrayed
ecstatic	confused
excited	frustrated
friendly	guilty
happy	hostile
important	ignorant
liked	jealous
loving	nervous
nice	obnoxious
pleased	overwhelmed
proud	sad
relieved	sarcastic
terrific	upset
thrilled	worried

In what ways are "You" messages and "I" messages two types of feeling statements?

"You" messages build trust. They focus on the other person's feelings. Some examples are:

- "You seem________________." Insert a feeling word in the blank, for example, "You seem confused."

"I" messages give feedback to the student. They focus on the speaker's feelings. For example:

- "I feel ____when you ______because_______________."
- You must be specific about an observable behavior, not express an attitude or a general impression.

There are two types of "I" messages:

- Compliments.
  - "Jill, I feel happy when you share your toy with Barbara because you both can play."
- Confrontations.
  - "Jill, I feel irritated when you take Barbara's pencil because it disturbs the class."

What are the pitfalls of complimenting and confronting "I" messages?

If the compliment is not directed to a specific act, it may be perceived as insincere.

Confrontation won't work unless you have some sort of trust relationship with the student.

But what if you're wrong about the student's feelings?

You are still genuinely trying to understand the student.

The student will correct you if you are wrong, but in any case, will appreciate your concern.

How can you acknowledge a person's contribution without evaluating or ignoring it?

In order to move along in a group, classroom lesson, or counseling session, and to acknowledge a person's contribution without evaluating or ignoring it, say:

- "Thanks for sharing … "
- "All right."
- "OK."
- "Thanks."

How can you bridge a response in a group-counseling or classroom-guidance situation?

You can bridge a response by:

- Calling attention to similarities and differences among student responses, which creates a sense of commonality and togetherness.

Two types of responses are:

- Bridging ideas or facts.
    - "Jane and Lori, you both seem to really like music."
- Bridging feelings.
    - "Jane and Lori, you both seem eager to tryout for the school band."

Summary:

Your goal as a counselor is to build relationships based on mutual sharing and feedback, in which your clients feel safe, and free of evaluation and judgment. This enables them to explore alternative ways to solve their own problems and take responsibility for their actions.

The goal of all communication is to be understood by others. The skills outlined in this chapter serve to build trust and understanding between counselors and students.

People don't care how much you know, until you show how much you care.
~ William Purkey

CHAPTER 3

INDIVIDUAL COUNSELING

What is counseling?

Counseling is:

- A process of interaction between the counselor and student.
- Goal-directed with the goal being the student's positive change in behavior.
- Confidential—the rights of students are always paramount.
- A learning process for students so that they will know they:
  - Have choices.
  - Can act on their choices.
  - Must take responsibility for their actions.
  - Must solve their own problems.

Counseling is not:

- A quick fix.
- Therapy.
- Advice-giving.
- Judgmental.
- The counselor solving problems for the student.
- Shared with others.

What will cause a "stranger" to confide in you?

Your use of communication skills (especially feeling statements) will engender trust.

Your visibility around school and your image as a friendly adult on the kids' side engenders trust.

Your follow-through with students will build confidence.

Your non-judgmental empathy and acceptance is reflected by enthusiasm and belief in the student as one who has made a mistake, not one who is a bad person.

Who will refer students to you?

Several possible referral sources are:

- Teachers.
- Parents.
- Child him/herself.
- Other school staff.

How will students be referred to you?

Students will be referred by:

- Verbal request.
  - This is when you have nothing in writing.
  - This is the usual way for parents to contact the counselor.

- Self-referral.
    - This allows students to bypass adult authority figures and come directly to the counselor.
- Written *Teacher Referral Form* (see page 36).
    - This is the best way for teacher referrals as it gives the counselor some background information on the student and situation.

What about the times a student is sent to you with a scribbled note, such as, "I've had it. He won't follow the rules. Something has to be done about his attitude."

See the student, but insist (after clearing with your principal) that a short referral form be completed for each teacher-initiated request for counseling (*Teacher Referral Form*, page 36).

What about confidentiality and legal concerns?

Legally, the law says children under a certain age do not have privacy rights. Such rights belong to their parents. This can make life difficult for the counselor. It is important to know what the legal age for privacy rights is in your state and/or school district.

The Ethical Standards for School Counselors, as defined by the American School Counselors Association, states in part, "... protects the confidentiality of information received in the counseling process ..."

However, ethical standards and legal requirements are not the same thing.

What do ethical and legal requirements mean to you, the counselor?

Confidentiality is an ethical, not a legal, concept.

Legally there are times you may have to divulge the contents of counseling sessions, specifically when:

- The client is a danger to him/herself or others.
- A court orders the release of information.
- Parents insist on knowing what their child discussed. Privacy rights of children belong legally with their parents until the legal age spelled out by your state and/or school district. Custodial and non-custodial parents share this right equally unless it is spelled out differently in a court order.

▶ How can you protect the privacy of your student clients?

You can:

- Inform them of the situations when you have to tell others what has been said: when you might hurt yourself, when someone else might hurt you, or you are in danger.
- Inform parents that the counseling sessions are confidential. Seek advice from your principal if pressured. School counselors do not have "privileged communication" protection in most states.
- Attend workshops and read books and articles to be informed. An excellent resource is *Ethical and Legal Issues In School Counseling Class*, by Huey and Remley.
- Use the general guideline of only sharing information on a "need to know" basis, and even then only the general areas of discussion.

▶ What are some ways to get started with a student client?

Use an *Initial Interview Form* (see pages 37-38) or or *Intake Form* (see page 39) which:

- Organizes the process of change.
- Is a plan of action that allows the tracking of goals/efforts and saves time.
- Is a good source of data for possible referral to a school Child Study Team committee or student-study committee.
- Is a more professional approach.

Using *Incomplete Sentences* (see page 40) for students to answer as part of the intake form is helpful. They not only serve as an icebreaker but also reveal thinking patterns.

How formal should the plan of action be?

This depends on the student. With some students, it may help to outline details on paper. You'll probably do this for yourself as the counselor anyway.

In any case:

- Set attainable goals to be accomplished and behaviors to be changed.
- Encourage and reinforce improvement.
- Pave the way, if possible, through consulting with teachers and/or parents so they are also looking for improvement and change over time. Do not expect a miraculous overnight cure!

Use the *Professional Plan Of Action* (see page 41).

What procedure should be used for individual counseling?

In the first session:

1. Arrange your office in a friendly, non-threatening, inviting way.
2. Remember to lean-in, use eye contact, and listen. Don't rush—counseling is a process that takes time, it is not a one-shot fix.
3. At first use mostly feeling statements to help build a relationship and mutual trust.
4. Unless the session is student-initiated, it is usually best to state why the student has been referred to you. For example, "I understand from Mrs. Wilson that you are having difficulty keeping your hands to yourself in her class. She is concerned about you and asked me to speak with you. What can you tell me about Mrs. Wilson's class?" and so on ...
5. Complete the *Initial Interview Form* (see pages 37-38) or *Intake Form* (see page 39).
6. Use the *Incomplete Sentences* (see page 40) as openers for your questions now or in session two.
7. Remember your priority is to build a relationship in order to explore alternative behaviors later. Don't be a detective—focus on the two "F's," *Feelings* and *Facts*.
8. Use role-playing and drawing as two non-threatening ways for students to share what they are concerned about. Many students like to role-play using puppets.
9. See page 42 for two activities (*Umbrella Activity* and *Shield Activity*) that can help build your relationship with the student.
10. Summarize (better yet, have the student summarize) what his/her problem is.

Prior to second session:

- Gather assessment data (formal and/or informal) by one or more of the following methods:
    - Speak with the referral source and share initial impressions—do not disclose confidential information.
    - Talk with the parent(s).
    - Schedule a conference with yourself and the parent, teacher, or both.

In intermediate sessions:

- Review the first session. Define the problem(s) and your recollection of the feelings about the problem(s).
- Follow the problem-solving process listed under "How do you systematically help students solve a problem?" (see below).
- Remember: The presenting problem may just be the tip of the iceberg or not a problem at all. For example, a student who constantly hits others may be a victim of abuse at home or reacting actively, rather than passively, to a divorce.
- Make plans to see the student at least once or twice a week for continuity and reinforcement purposes, but usually not more than six times.

Some hints about the closure or termination of counseling:

- When the student has made sufficient progress toward solving or alleviating his/her problem(s), it is important to continue checking on the student, in an informal or nonscheduled way.
- Stickers, *Happygrams* (see page 43), etc. help foster the new-found behaviors.
- A relapse or reappearance of a behavior does not mean you, the counselor, have somehow failed. It may mean that the student's method of dealing with certain problems has led to new concerns or problems. For example, after a divorce experience, sometimes children will confront parents, and parents have difficulty dealing with this.
- Remember: You don't have time to do extensive individual counseling. Six sessions are about the maximum for most students.
- Focus on changes the student can make at school. You can't control his/her environment and home-related problems. Your goal is to teach problem-solving strategies that can generalize to other situations.
- If the student needs additional help, the parent(s) may wish to take him/her for counseling/therapy outside the school.

▶ How do you systematically help students solve a problem?

You help students by teaching them the following problem-solving process. Have them:

- Define the problem in behavioral terms.
- Describe their feelings about the problem.
- Review the steps they have already used to try to solve the problem.
- Explore what they could try (possible actions) and what might happen (possible consequences, pro or con).
- Develop a plan:
  - What will you do?
  - Who else is involved (if anyone)?
  - Where will it start?
  - When will it start?
  - How will you start the plan?
- Review progress (set a date and time for the review).

It is important to remember that the essence of the problem-solving process is to teach the students that all choices have consequences and they are responsible for the consequences of their actions.

What is behavior modification contracting?

Behavior modification is one of the most common strategies used with individual counseling. It should not be used if the teacher is not in favor of it.

Behavior modification can be helpful when it is used initially to get students "on the right track."

One caution is that heavy reliance on behavior modification may lead to dependence on external rewards for appropriate behavior.

When it is used, a gradual fading of reinforcement needs to occur in order to decrease dependence on you or the rewards.

Emphasis must be on the student's learning to manage his/her own behavior. Making successful responsible choices are motivating as well.

The *Behavior Contract* (see pages 44-45) can be used to monitor a student's behavior at school.

The *Behavior Modification Chart* (see page 46) is another example of a form that can be used to monitor a student's behavior at school.

A *Sample Behavior Modification Plan* (see page 47) outlines how one parent effectively implemented behavior modification at home.

The *Citizenship Report* (see page 48) is an example of a report sent home to the parents of a student concerning behavior modification in the classroom. It could also be used with any plan because it serves as a vehicle for communication between the school and the parents.

Behavior modification chart explanation:

In the example chart on page 34, Joe must earn 6 points per day to earn a daily reward.

- On Monday, Wednesday, and Thursday, he did not earn the minimum 6 points (teacher rates him right before lunch and at the end of the day).
- On Tuesday and Friday, he did earn a pseudo dollar.
- Joe brings his chart to the counselor daily for a pseudo dollar if he has earned it or to discuss what he has not done to earn the dollar.
- On Fridays, Joe gets to spend his dollars on trinkets or small rewards which cost one or more pseudo dollars.

Adams Elementary School
Behavior Expectation For Joe James
Period M-F Jan. 5-9

BEHAVIORS	POINTS	MON	TUE	WED	THU	FRI
Stays in Seat	1 am	1	1	0	1	1
	1 pm	1	1	1	1	1
Raises Hand Before Speaking	1 am	0	1	0	1	1
	1 pm	1	0	1	0	1
Keeps Hands To Self	1 am	0	1	0	1	1
	1 pm	0	0	0	0	0
Completes Work	1 am	1	1	0	0	1
	1 pm	0	1	0	0	1
		4	6	2	4	7

If Joe earns 6 points during the daily period,
He will earn 1 Adams dollar (to be used on trinkets or small rewards).

Joe James   Mr. Burgess

But what if the teacher doesn't want to take time to fill out the chart?

Have the teacher send the student to you at the end of each day with a note saying whether or not the dollar was earned. This is not as precise, but the teacher is still part of the change process, which is the key element.

The rest of the procedure remains the same.

Summary:

People's capacity to change their behavior always rests on three premises:

1. They have to want to change (improve) their situation.
2. People must solve their own problems. You cannot do it for them.
3. Change must be built on success, not failure. It is always easy to see a student's faults. What is not so easy is to see positive steps for dealing with ways to change these faults.

This is why self-esteem is so important. Your students and counselees must be able to see the possibility of success—however slight—in order to attempt to change. Your job is to build in "small wins." Small successes in changing behavior (This is where your support and encouragement is vital.) are needed in order to tackle the larger changes later. The chances for success, of course, increase when incentives occur at home and school.

TEACHER REFERRAL FORM

Student: ______________________________

Referred by: ______________________________

Problems/Issues: ______________________________

____

____

Please check items student displays:

Academic behaviors

- ☐ Does not participate in class
- ☐ Poor study habits
- ☐ Does not complete homework
- ☐ Does not complete class work
- ☐ Anxious while taking tests
- ☐ Disorganized
- ☐ Does not follow directions
- ☐ Does not pay attention

Self-understanding

- ☐ Poor decision-making skills
- ☐ Lacks self-confidence
- ☐ Negative communication skills
- ☐ Lacks self-control
- ☐ Poor anger management skills
- ☐ Poor goal-setting habits

Relationships with others:

- ☐ Poor social skills
- ☐ Teased by others
- ☐ Teases other students
- ☐ Lacks positive friendships
- ☐ Not aware of the feelings of others
- ☐ Negative family relationships
- ☐ Poor problem-solving skills
- ☐ Does not work well in groups

Check any behavior that the child frequently displays in class:

☐ Happy	☐ Anxious	☐ Sad
☐ Withdrawn	☐ Angry	☐ Worrisome
☐ Sleepy		

☐ ______________________________

☐ ______________________________

Please elaborate on any of the areas you marked, so I can have a fuller understanding. (If you need more space, please write on the back side of this sheet.)

One positive thing about this student:

WHEN YOU FINISH THIS FORM, PLEASE DROP THIS FORM IN MY MAILBOX.

I will contact you to arrange a time for me to meet with this student. Thanks for all your help!

INITIAL INTERVIEW FORM

Find in cumulative folder:

Name of student:________________________________ Date of birth: ________________________

Age:__________ Grade: __________

Previous counseling:

Medical history:____

____

____

____

Medication currently taking: ____

____

____

Significant developmental events: ____

____

____

Grades: ____

Emergency contact information:

Name:______________________________________ Phone number: (________) ____________________

To be filled out by the client with the counselor:

What do you do for fun (interests/hobbies)?____

____

What do you think you are good at doing (your strengths)? _________________________________

____

Whom do you live with? ____

How do you get along with those that you live with? _______________________________________

____

How are your grades?____

What do you need help with? ____

____

How do you get along with your classmates?____

____

How well do you make and keep friends? ____

____

Which word describes how you feel most of the time?

☐ Happy ☐ Frustrated ☐ Angry
☐ Sad ☐ Worried ☐ Cheerful
☐ Other ____

What made you choose this word?____

Why do you think ____________________ thought that you should talk to me?
(REFERRED BY)

Is that a problem you would like me to help you with? ____________________

What problem(s) would *you* like me to help you with? (If different from above) ____________________

____

Tell me more about this problem(s). ____

____

____

Have you ever tried to solve this problem before? ____________________

If yes, what did you do? ____

____

If the problem was solved, what would be different? ____________________
What is the goal? ____

What are some things you could do to get closer to solving the problem (reaching the goal)? ________

____

____

INTAKE FORM

NAME ______________________ DATE ______________________

AGE ______________________ GRADE ______________________

TEACHER ______________________ ROOM # ______________________

PROBLEM/CONCERN FROM REFERRAL SOURCE: ______________________

____

____

____

____

STUDENT'S PERCEPTION OF PROBLEM(S): ______________________

____

____

____

____

STUDENT'S FEELINGS:

Things I like about myself: ______________________

____

____

Things I don't like about myself: ______________________

____

____

PLAN OF ACTION: *(Include what she/he is to do and timelines)* ______________________

____

____

____

____

____

REVIEW DATE: ______________________

INCOMPLETE SENTENCES

Complete each sentence with the first thing that comes to your mind.

1. Most of all, I want ______________________________________ .
2. I'm afraid ______________________________________ .
3. My father ______________________________________ .
4. I know I can ______________________________________ .
5. I worry about ______________________________________ .
6. My mother always ______________________________________ .
7. My mother never ______________________________________ .
8. I'm different from others because ______________________________________ .
9. When I get mad, ______________________________________ .
10. Teachers ______________________________________ .
11. I want to know ______________________________________ .
12. Teachers think I ______________________________________ .
13. Kids think I ______________________________________ .
14. When I grow up, ______________________________________ .
15. I wish I were ______________________________________ .

PROFESSIONAL PLAN OF ACTION

Student's Name: ____________________

CUMULATIVE RECORD

Achievement Tests __________

Ability Tests __________

Other Pertinent Information:

____

____

____

TYPE OF CONTACT

- ☐ Class observation
- ☐ Individual counseling session
- ☐ Parent contact
- ☐ Letter from home
- ☐ Child-study team meeting
- ☐ Conference with teacher
- ☐ Testing/screening
- ☐ Other: __________

Comments: __________

____

____

FOLLOW-UP

- ☐ None at this time
- ☐ Follow progress
- ☐ Contact parents
  Previous contacts by teacher? ☐ yes ☐ no
- ☐ Test/screen
  ☐ WRAT ☐ SIT ☐ Other __________
- ☐ Discuss with:
  ☐ Child-study team __________ (DATE) ☐ Teacher __________ (DATE)
- ☐ Refer to __________ Check back date __________
- ☐ Give suggestions to teacher and monitor Behavior Modification Charts
- ☐ Contact outside agency/person __________
  Phone number __________ Date contacted __________
- ☐ Home visit
- ☐ Discuss with principal __________ (DATE)
- ☐ Individual sessions
- ☐ Small-group counseling
  Type of group __________ Starting date __________
- ☐ Other: __________

Comments: __________

____

____

UMBRELLA ACTIVITY

This activity can be used with students who experience irrational thoughts or students who think negatively about themselves or situations.

MATERIALS:

- ☐ 2 pieces of construction paper (different colors)
- ☐ Scissors
- ☐ Pen/pencil/markers
- ☐ Glue stick

PRIOR TO ACTIVITY:

Write down the irrational/negative thoughts the student is experiencing. Help the student think of rational/positive thoughts to replace these irrational/negative ones.

STUDENT INSTRUCTIONS:

1. Draw an umbrella on one of the pieces of construction paper.
2. Divide the umbrella into the number of parts equal to the number of negative thoughts the student has expressed. *(If the student has 3 negative thoughts, then divide the umbrella into 3 parts.)*
3. Using the same piece of paper, have the student draw the same number of raindrops as parts of the umbrella.
4. Cut out the raindrops and the umbrella.
5. Glue the umbrella to the lower half and raindrops to the upper half of the other piece of construction paper.
6. Write an irrational/negative thought on each raindrop.
7. Write the corresponding rational/positive thoughts on the umbrella.

QUESTIONS TO ASK THE STUDENTS:

1. What is the purpose of an umbrella? *(To shield people from the rain)*
2. What is the purpose of rational/positive thoughts? *(To eliminate irrational/negative thinking.)*
3. How does the umbrella help to eliminate irrational/negative thinking? *(It stops irrational/negative thinking from taking over one's thoughts.)*

SHIELD ACTIVITY

This activity can be used with students who are in unfortunate situations over which they have no control.

MATERIALS:

- ☐ Piece of construction paper
- ☐ Markers/Crayons

STUDENT INSTRUCTIONS:

1. Draw a shield.
2. Divide the shield into 4 parts.
3. In each section, have the student draw or write something that is going well in his/her life, something he/she enjoys doing, or something he/she feels he/she does well.

QUESTIONS TO ASK THE STUDENTS:

1. What is the purpose of a shield? *(to protect people)*
2. At what times could you think about this shield?

HAPPYGRAM

School was brighter
today because

____

has shown
improvement
in respecting others
and
in following our rules.

____

GUIDANCE COUNSELOR

BEHAVIOR CONTRACT

Made Between

_________________________ and _________________________

beginning on

______/______/______.

The behaviors I am agreeing to show:

1. ____

2. ____

3. ____

If I do these things in class, I will receive:

At School: ____

____

At Home: ____

____

Student's signature: ______________________________

Teacher's signature: ______________________________

Parent's signature ______________________________

Counselor's signature: ______________________________

Once the contract is signed, explain the chart below to the students. Inform them that each week the chart will be taped to the desk. Whenever they reach their goal in the morning or the afternoon, they will receive a point (smiley faces or stickers may be used too). In order to receive the school and home incentive, they need to earn a set number of points for the week. (For the first time, it is important to set an easily attainable number, for we want the students to feel successful.) Let them know that the number will increase every few weeks.

On Fridays, instruct the classroom teacher to send the chart home.

GOAL:

	MONDAY	TUESDAY	WEDNESDAY	THURSDAY	FRIDAY
MORNING					
AFTERNOON					

BEHAVIOR MODIFICATION CHART

____ School

Behavior Expectation For_______________________ Period _________

BEHAVIORS	POINTS	MON	TUE	WED	THU	FRI
	1 am					
______________________	1 pm					
	1 am					
______________________	1 pm					
	1 am					
______________________	1 pm					
	1 am					
______________________	1 pm					
	Total Points	_____	_____	_____	_____	_____

If ___________________________ earns _______ points during the ______ period, he/she will earn ____.

______________________ STUDENT

______________________ COUNSELOR

To:___________________________

Please monitor ___________________________ for the behavior(s) he/she agreed to change. Give one (1) point for satisfactory morning behavior in each area and one (1) point for satisfactory afternoon behavior in each area. Give no (0) points for unsatisfactory behavior.

Please send him/her to see me daily at _______________ am/pm for the length of the contract.

______________________ GUIDANCE COUNSELOR

SAMPLE BEHAVIOR MODIFICATION PLAN
(PARENT)

This plan was developed by a parent to meet the specific needs of her child. It has been used by many other parents with great success. Of course, changes are made to meet the particular needs of each child and family situation. It has provisions for immediate reinforcement as well as long-term rewards for the child to work toward.

HOMEWORK—DONE NEATLY AND CORRECTLY

1. Each assignment—3 points
2. Weekly spelling test—Improved grade
   - A—3 points
   - B—2 points
   - C—1 point
3. Assignment book signed by teacher—1 point

POINTS MAY BE USED AS FOLLOWS:

Watch TV for one hour—4 points

1. Cartoons—Monday
2. Favorite TV Show—Tuesday
3. Favorite TV Show—Sunday

Someone to spend the night—30 points (once every 3 months)

School skating party—20 points (once each month)

Choose the place we go to eat—20 points

1. McDonald's
2. Burger King
3. Pizza Hut
4. Taco Bell
5. TGI Fridays

Go to a friend's house to play—4 points (for one hour)

For maximum effectiveness, both the parent and the child should be involved when setting up the plan. It is useful to have a sample to hand to parents to help them get started.

CITIZENSHIP REPORT ON ______________________ PERIOD __________

Your child is expected to demonstrate the following correct behaviors during the period above.

KEY

Satisfactory **I**mproving **N**eeds to improve

	MON	TUE	WED	THU	FRI
Be In Seat On Time					
Have Paper, Pencil, And Ready To Work					
Be Quiet While Teacher Is Giving Directions					
Follow Directions					
Complete All Work					
Work Quietly					
Stay In Seat					
Raise Hand Before Speaking					
Keep Hands To Him/Herself					
Other					

Please Sign And Return Tomorrow.

Please make any comments on the back

Date	Teacher Signature	Parent Signature
________	______________________	______________________
________	______________________	______________________
________	______________________	______________________
________	______________________	______________________
________	______________________	______________________

CHAPTER 4

SMALL-GROUP COUNSELING

What is the difference between small-group counseling and classroom guidance?

Both are direct services to students; however, they are not the same.

COUNSELING IS A PROCESS	CLASSROOM GUIDANCE IS A LESSON
Usually less than 10 members.	Entire classroom (15 or more).
Leader facilitates communication among members.	Leader presents information.
Atmosphere of openness, trust, support.	Atmosphere of information giving and processing.
Leader is a certified school counselor.	Leader may be a teacher, principal, counselor, etc.
Techniques are largely verbal—interaction is the key process.	Techniques run the gamut of approaches—basically is teaching.

What is the purpose of small-group counseling?

Small-group counseling helps students learn to explore with others their attitudes, ideas, feelings, and how these are related to their behaviors.

What is it that makes small-group counseling such an effective intervention?

Small-group counseling is effective because, no matter what the reason for forming the group, it allows:

- The processes of listening and speaking to occur in a non-judgmental setting.
- Self-disclosure.
- An opportunity to be listened to.
- Giving and receiving feedback from one's peers to take place.

It allows students to listen to other students, and gives the counselor insight into student interactions. Additionally, it can be very enlightening for students to "see" that others have similar concerns—"I am not the only one."

How do I get students into my group?

Students become a part of group counseling through:

- Counselor recommendation. While working with individuals you may feel that a small-group experience is appropriate.
- Parent requests.
- Teacher suggestions.

What are some ways to solicit for groups?

Announce the formation of groups in a school newsletter or other flyer that goes home to parents. A modification of a parent notification letter can be used as an announcement (see sample *Parental Notification Letter,* page 56).

Visit the classrooms and give the students (who can read) simple outlines of the groups available. After receiving the teacher's permission to do so, ask the students to volunteer for the groups they would be interested in. When offering self-referral groups, be careful not to allow students to select more groups than you have time to conduct. If this happens, the students will be disappointed and you may feel guilty.

Provide teachers with the *Student Behavior Rating Scale* (see page 57) to help them identify students who are possible group counseling candidates.

If special interest groups such as a group for divorce/separation are to be formed, visit each classroom and explain, in general, the nature of the group. Have the interested students write their names on slips of paper and give these to the teacher, who will then give them to the counselor.

- Hint: For divorce/separation groups, interview the potential participants first, and at that time, give them permission forms for a parent signature.
- Send a copy of the explanatory letter (see page 58) to the teacher.

Do I need parental permission to run groups?

Although it is always a sound professional approach to provide a parental notification letter, whether or not parent permission is required depends on the policy of your local school district. Upon completion of the group, it is a good practice to notify parents (see sample notification of completion letter, page 59).

How do you organize groups?

Groups are organized based on the common needs or concerns of the members. For example, students who are:

- Potential leaders.
- From divorced or alcoholic families.
- Aggressive.
- Shy.
- Underachieving.
- Low in self image.
- Facing or experiencing the death of a loved one.

How often should groups meet and for how long?

Groups should be scheduled:

- Generally once a week for 30 minutes for six sessions. (There is a sample schedule in Chapter 8, page 156).

What and how many rules do I need for the group?

Rules are important, but should be kept to a minimum. Rules may be decided on by either the leader, students, or both.

Some examples of rules are:

- One student speaks at a time.
- Any student may pass at any time.
- Students will keep private what is said in the group setting.

How do I keep teachers informed of what's happening in the groups without breaking confidentiality?

Give the teacher a weekly report which notes the progress you see in the students, but does not tell specific details about the counseling sessions.

Since most referrals come from teachers, how can I control and guide this process?

First, decide what kinds of groups you can provide, then let the teachers know what the groups are and the goals of each group.

Ask the teachers to give you the names of the students whom they feel could benefit from small-group counseling of a particular type. (For an example of a *Teacher Referral Form*, see page 36.)

What are the goals for decision-making/problem-solving groups?

The goals for a decision-making or problem-solving group are to:

- Generate alternative ways to handle problems other than physical aggression.
- Make decisions based on possible consequences of one's actions.
- Take responsibility for actions regardless of the consequences of those actions.
- Perceive how others view one's actions.
- Experience positive interaction with others.
- Learn how a student's thoughts about him/herself and his/her abilities influence behavior.

What are the goals for peer relationship groups?

The goals for a peer relationship group are to:

- Experience positive interactions with others.
- Learn that each person has special strengths, skills, abilities, feelings, and needs.

- Learn how a student's thoughts about him/herself and his/her abilities influence behavior.
- Learn how others perceive one's behavior.

What are the goals for self-concept groups?

The goals for a self-concept group are to:

- Recognize one's ability to interact with others.
- Value one's own personal strengths, skills, abilities, feelings, and needs.
- Learn how one's thoughts about oneself influence behavior.
- Learn how others perceive one's behavior.

What are the goals for divorce/separation/remarriage groups?

The goals for a divorce/separation/remarriage group are to:

- Identify and clarify students' feelings and behaviors concerning their parents' situation.
- Help students gain a realistic picture of the situation and make effective decisions.
- Give students an opportunity to learn new communication and coping skills.
- Help students discover the positive aspects of their unique situations.

What are the goals for communication groups?

The goals for a communication group are to:

- Practice and improve listening skills.
- Develop a basic feeling-word vocabulary.
- Learn to recognize, share, and accept feelings.
- Learn the relationship between positive choices, responsible behavior, and positive consequences.
- Differentiate between solvable and unsolvable problems.
- Differentiate between rational and irrational thoughts.

What are the goals for study-skills groups?

The goals for a study-skills group are to:

- Practice and improve listening skills.
- Learn specific time-management skills.
- Develop and practice organizational techniques for materials (see *How To Get Organized,* page 60).
- Acquire better test-preparation and test-taking skills (see *Testing Tips* page 61 and *Test Planning Sheet,* page 62).
- Learn a systematic approach for completing homework, including environment, scheduling, etc. (see *Homework,* page 63).
- Identify behaviors which interfere with school success and create a plan to modify these behaviors (see *Before You Study,* pages 64-65).

▶ **But I don't have time to get materials and develop different group plans for all the needy students in my school—where do I start?**

All group members need certain skills and understanding in order to benefit from a group experience. You can teach common skills to all groups.

▶ **What are the common skills and understandings that all group members need?**

All group members can learn to:

- Listen.
- Process feelings by:
  - Increasing their vocabulary of feeling words.
  - Sharing their feelings with other group members.
  - Understanding that feelings are tied to actions.
- Develop self-esteem by:
  - Being able to make choices.
  - Accepting the consequences of their actions.
  - Having responsible actions recognized.
- Improve communication skills by:
  - Understanding and using "I" messages.
  - Understanding and using "You" messages.
- Express trust and caring.

▶ **How much emphasis should be placed on these common skills and understandings?**

Since all group members need common skills and understandings, specific sessions dealing with these are a valuable part of a group plan. Remember, the process itself is as important as the content.

▶ **Is there one basic model which can be used to structure all groups?**

Yes. It would include:

- One or two introductory sessions (depending on the age of members).
- One closing session.
- In between the opening and closing sessions, there can be core content sessions based on the needs of the group.

An example of a communication group structured as a basic model can be found on pages 66-75, reproducible forms/worksheets for the sample model on pages 76-86.

▶ **How do I keep track of everybody in the group and everything going on in the group?**

Keep your records on the *Group Contact Sheet* (see page 87).

▶ Summary:

Your goal in group counseling is to help students learn that they can change their behavior in order to solve their own problems.

Students need to realize that all choices have consequences, both positive and negative.

Students should learn that human beings are good people who make mistakes and learn from them, and not bad people who are doomed to repeat their mistakes.

Through a combination of individual and small-group counseling (developmental or problem-oriented), students will learn to generate positive alternatives, to solve problems, and to take responsibility for their actions.

Results of group counseling should be shared with your principal and teachers. The *Pre- And Post-Assessment Evaluation Results* (see page 87) is provided as an example form that can be used for this purpose.

PARENTAL NOTIFICATION LETTER

Date ________________________________

Student's Name ________________________

Dear______________________________ ,

During the next few weeks, I will be conducting small-group counseling sessions with students experiencing academic and/or behavior problems in school which may be related to a marital change in the family, such as divorce or separation. That is, the child's adjustment to the family marital situation may not be as positive as it might be, and may be affecting his/her performance in school.

Your child may benefit from such a small-group experience. Each group is limited to six participants, and involves eight, thirty-minute sessions with the counselor during a four-week period.

Please be assured that this is not intended as an invasion of a family's privacy. The students are taught what confidentiality means at the first meeting. The objectives of this group are:

- To identify and clarify students' feelings and behaviors concerning their parents' divorces or separations.
- To help students gain a realistic picture of the divorce situation and make effective decisions.
- To give students an opportunity to learn new communication and coping skills.
- To help students discover the positive aspects of their unique situations.

In short, the advantages of a group of this kind are that a child can see that he/she is not the only one to whom this has happened, that there are many feelings involved on the part of everyone who is involved in the situation, that no one is "at fault," and whatever the home situation is, it is now a fact of life to which the child can learn to make a positive adjustment.

If you have any questions or concerns, please call me at (_______)_________________ .

Sincerely,

____
SCHOOL COUNSELOR

PLEASE MAKE YOUR CHOICE, SIGN, AND RETURN BY ______________

✄ ....

☐ **YES**, I want my child to participate in a divorce/separation group.

☐ **NO**, I do not want my child to participate in a divorce/separation group.

Child's name ______________________________

Signature ______________________________ Date ____________

STUDENT BEHAVIOR RATING SCALE

Student ______________________________ Date ______________

Teacher ______________________________ Grade ______________

The items below reflect problems which students may have. Please check once if you have noticed this student having this problem; check twice if the problem seems severe.

LEARNING

- ☐☐ Both ability and achievement severely below age expectations
- ☐☐ Significant discrepancy between ability and achievement
- ☐☐ Short attention span—difficulty concentrating
- ☐☐ Poor printing or writing—difficulty copying from board
- ☐☐ Difficulty following oral directions
- ☐☐ Forgets almost immediately what was seen or heard
- ☐☐ Confuses left from right or shows reversals in reading or writing
- ☐☐ Significant differences in reading, written expression, and/or math levels
- ☐☐ Difficulty learning a series such as the alphabet
- ☐☐ Difficulty learning and/or remembering ideas, facts, rules, or dates
- ☐☐ Excessive motor activity
- ☐☐ Significant difficulty with math concepts and computations
- ☐☐ Difficulty comprehending what is read

COMMUNICATION

- ☐☐ Has inadequate vocabulary for age level
- ☐☐ Experiences difficulty in expressing self in complete sentences
- ☐☐ Exhibits inaccurate grammatical use
- ☐☐ Has difficulty organizing ideas into logical sequence of events
- ☐☐ Has difficulty "finding" the exact word wanted
- ☐☐ Has difficulty recalling or relating precisely a past event or sequence
- ☐☐ Misunderstands the obvious intent of simple statements
- ☐☐ Uses gestures rather than words to express wants and needs
- ☐☐ Exhibits poor articulation skills
- ☐☐ Exhibits fluency problems (stuttering)
- ☐☐ Exhibits voice problems (intensity, pitch, intonation)

BEHAVIOR

- ☐☐ Blames others
- ☐☐ Bullies
- ☐☐ Teases
- ☐☐ Defiant
- ☐☐ Destroys property
- ☐☐ Dislikes school
- ☐☐ Disobedient
- ☐☐ Disruptive
- ☐☐ Easily angered
- ☐☐ Fights
- ☐☐ Lies
- ☐☐ Steals
- ☐☐ Swears
- ☐☐ Throws objects
- ☐☐ Anxious
- ☐☐ Attention-seeking
- ☐☐ Boisterous
- ☐☐ Cries easily
- ☐☐ Excitable
- ☐☐ Hypertensive
- ☐☐ Hypochondriac
- ☐☐ Noisy
- ☐☐ Out of seat
- ☐☐ Overactive
- ☐☐ Restless
- ☐☐ Tense
- ☐☐ Worries
- ☐☐ Daydreams
- ☐☐ Depressed
- ☐☐ Drowsy
- ☐☐ Easily confused
- ☐☐ Easily led
- ☐☐ Inattentive
- ☐☐ Loner
- ☐☐ Overly shy
- ☐☐ Preoccupied
- ☐☐ Quits easily
- ☐☐ Slow worker
- ☐☐ Uncooperative
- ☐☐ Unmotivated
- ☐☐ Clumsy
- ☐☐ Dependent
- ☐☐ Distractible
- ☐☐ Energetic
- ☐☐ Impulsive
- ☐☐ Immature
- ☐☐ Inflexible
- ☐☐ Interrupts
- ☐☐ Irresponsible
- ☐☐ Moody
- ☐☐ Self-conscious
- ☐☐ Shows off
- ☐☐ Temper tantrums

Describe additional behaviors ____

____

____

Date _______________

Dear __________________________________,

The student(s) listed below from your class has (have) shown interest in participating in a divorce/separation/remarriage group called C.H.O.I.C.E.

________________________ ________________________
________________________ ________________________
________________________ ________________________
________________________ ________________________
________________________ ________________________

The purpose of our group is to improve self-understanding and to help each student with personal day-to-day problems.

Improvement, as you know, is frequently slow because children in divorce situations often simultaneously lose both their confidence and their security. School may not be a priority for them because they can't concentrate due to anxiety and guilt feelings.

A successful group provides peer support, acknowledges feelings, and improves self-understanding. The group is designed to help each student be more successful in school by dealing with home factors that may Interfere with school success.

C HILDREN
H ELPING
O THERS
I N A
C ARING
E NVIRONMENT

Sincerely,

____
SCHOOL COUNSELOR

P.S. I'll contact you about times and days for group meetings.

Date ________________

Dear __________________________________,

Your child has recently completed a small-group counseling experience designed to improve his/her confidence, the ability to interact with others, the ability to make decisions, and to learn what taking responsibility for one's actions really means.

As a parent, please remember that you are your child's primary and most important teacher. As such, remember to "catch him/her doing good" and, when you do, give a positive comment. Also, try to remember in the heat of negative situations and feelings, that your aim is not just to remedy the problem at hand, but to teach your child how to deal with his/her feelings, develop choices, make decisions, and accept responsibility for his/her actions. You teach constantly through the behavior you model for your child. What you do shows your child what he/she should do.

Your goal and ours is to help your child "to be the best he/she can be."

I have taken the liberty to enclose pamphlets which you may be able to use. There are also many community resources available if you wish further assistance. I would be glad to recommend additional resources. Please feel free to contact me at (_________) ___________________ .

Sincerely,

____

SCHOOL COUNSELOR

HOW TO GET ORGANIZED

☑ **THINK AHEAD**

What are you going to be doing?
What will you need?

☑ **BE READY FOR THE DAY**

Have the right supplies.
Know where your supplies can be found.

☑ **MAKE A LIST**

Write down what you need to do.

☑ **PRIORITIZE**

Decide the order in which the things on your list should be completed.
Chores? Homework? TV? Friends? Practice? Snack?

☑ **KNOW HOW MUCH TIME YOU HAVE**

☑ **BREAK BIG JOBS INTO SMALL JOBS**

☑ **GET STARTED! DON'T WASTE TIME!**

☑ **STAY ON TRACK!**

Avoid people and places that can distract you.
Avoid anything that takes your attention away from your work.

☑ **CHECK YOUR WORK**

Look for careless mistakes. You may have skipped a problem.

☑ **KNOW WHEN YOU ARE FINISHED**

Checklist:

- ☐ I have done all the problems I can.
- ☐ I believe all my answers are correct.
- ☐ My handwriting is neat.
- ☐ I have checked my punctuation and grammar.

TESTING TIPS

All Year Long:
Attend school, pay attention,
complete homework assignments,
and practice flashcards on a daily basis.

A Week Prior To The Test:
Have time put aside daily to have some fun
and get some exercise.

The Night Before The Test:
Get a good night's rest.

The Night Before The Test And The Day Of The Test:
Eat a healthy dinner and breakfast (avoid sugar).

The Morning Of The Test:
Get up extra early so you do not have to worry
about being late for school.

The Morning Of The Test:
Make sure you pack extra #2 pencils.

The Morning Of The Test:
Go to school prepared to do your **best!**

TEST PLANNING SHEET

3 DAY RULE
You must start
studying 3 days
before the test!

TO PREPARE FOR A TEST DO ANY OR ALL OF THE FOLLOWING:

- ☑ Make flashcards and play a game.
- ☑ Read aloud your notes to yourself.
- ☑ Write down important information again.
- ☑ Draw helpful pictures and diagrams.
- ☑ Read the pages that will be covered in the test.

STUDY CALENDAR

WEEK OF ________________

MONDAY	TUESDAY	WEDNESDAY

THURSDAY	FRIDAY	SATURDAY	SUNDAY

HOMEWORK

- ☑ Listen In Class.
- ☑ Write Down Your Assignments.
- ☑ Pack The Right Supplies.
- ☑ Have A Good Study Space At Home.
- ☑ Set Aside The Time You Need.
- ☑ Check Off Your Assignments When Completed.
- ☑ Pack Your Bookbag For The Next Day.

Fill in the chart below with each subject that you have for homework in the time slot that you plan to complete that assignment. Don't forget to write in other activities such as dinner, soccer practice, etc.

	3:00	4:00	5:00	6:00	7:00	8:00	9:00
MON							
TUE							
WED							
THU							
FRI							

BEFORE YOU STUDY...

	OFTEN	SOMETIMES	RARELY
LIFESTYLE			
I spend too much time watching TV and/or listening to music.	☐	☐	☐
I get plenty of exercise.	☐	☐	☐
I get at least eight hours of sleep a night.	☐	☐	☐
I eat a well-balanced diet, including breakfast.	☐	☐	☐
ASSIGNMENTS			
I write down each assignment on an assignment pad/sheet of notebook paper.	☐	☐	☐
I ask my teacher questions if I don't understand.	☐	☐	☐
I use the buddy system by having a friend I can call if I don't understand assignments when I get home.	☐	☐	☐
SCHEDULE			
I keep a schedule that shows a regular time to study.	☐	☐	☐
I put off doing assignments.	☐	☐	☐
If I don't have any assignments, I use that time to read.	☐	☐	☐
I think how long each assignment will take and do my best to stick to that schedule.	☐	☐	☐
I spend too much time on one assignment.	☐	☐	☐
If I have a test coming up, I spread my studying out over several days.	☐	☐	☐
PLACE			
I have a regular place to study that is quiet, comfortable, and has good lighting.	☐	☐	☐

OVER →

	OFTEN	SOMETIMES	RARELY
ORGANIZATION			
I put my books in the same place so I can always find them.	☐	☐	☐
Before I start an assignment, I clear my desk of all the things I do not need.	☐	☐	☐
I have the things I may need—pencils, ruler, eraser, dictionary, notebooks, worksheets, books.	☐	☐	☐

WHILE STUDYING...

FOCUS			
Before I start, I think about what I already know about the topic.	☐	☐	☐
I stop and ask myself questions. Make flashcards.	☐	☐	☐
I make a "To Do" list and reward myself with stars and checks when I complete an assignment.	☐	☐	☐
I take a short five-minute break between studying for each subject.	☐	☐	☐
I make charts, lists, or outlines to organize my thoughts. (Make a word puzzle.)	☐	☐	☐

AFTER STUDYING...

REVIEW			
I think about how what I have learned fits with what I already know.	☐	☐	☐
I retell what I learned to a parent or a friend or I make a tape of myself and replay it.	☐	☐	☐
I ask my parents or friends to ask me questions.	☐	☐	☐

COMMUNICATION GROUP MODEL

INTRODUCTORY NOTES:

The purpose is to improve each student's ability to communicate.

Any given session's plan should not take precedence over the members' processing.

The concluding plan of action (POA), which is to be carried out by each group member and reviewed at the start of the next session, is intended to provide continuity between the sessions.

Parent notification or permission for a student's participation is vital. Always inform parents in writing of the group's goals and objectives, and give some suggestions for parent follow-up activities when the group is concluded. (For a sample parental notification/permission form, see page 56 and a follow-up letter for parents, see page 59.)

Teacher understanding and support for small-group counseling is essential. Teachers should be kept informed of their students' progress, perhaps through a pre- and post-assessment of behaviors related to learning (see *Evaluation Questions For Group Communication Model,* page 76). Likewise, the principal should be apprised of the group's activities.

OBJECTIVES FOR THE COMMUNICATION GROUP MODEL:

Session 1:

1. Explain why the group is meeting.
2. Learn the names of each group member.
3. Provide an opportunity for all members to share.
4. Present the group rules.
5. Practice listening.

Session 2:

1. Develop a basic feeling-word vocabulary.
2. Recognize, accept, and share feelings.

Session 3:

1. Review and develop a feeling-word vocabulary.
2. Understand and apply a "You" message.

Session 4:

1. Review and add to the feeling-word vocabulary.
2. Review a "You" message.
3. Understand and apply an "I" message.

Core content sessions may or may not be included with this model at the discretion of the counselor. (Model may be used alone to improve communication skills of the members or the skills learned can be combined with a specific focus, e.g., divorce adjustment, making friends, etc.)

Following Core-Content Sessions:

1. Review the skills and understandings learned to date.
2. Differentiate between solvable and unsolvable problems.

Session ( ) (For ages 9 and older):

1. Differentiate between rational and irrational thoughts.

Final Session:

1. Conclude the group experience in a positive manner.
2. Have each group member hear positive statements from other members.
3. Learn the concept of validation.
4. Members evaluate the group experience.

SESSION 1:

A. Objectives:

1. To explain why the group is meeting.
2. To learn the names of each group member.
3. To give an opportunity for all members to share.
4. To learn the group rules.
5. To practice listening.
6. To learn the importance of listening.

B. Target Group (by age): 6-8 years old or 9-12 years old.

C. Time Requirement: 30-40 minutes (all sessions).

D. Materials: Copy of *Evaluation Questions For Communication Group Model* (see page 76) and a pencil for each student.

E. Procedure:

1. Introduce yourself and your "helper" if you wish (which could be a puppet).
2. Explain the purpose of the group in simple terms. For example: "Several students have talked to me about ______ , so we decided to have a group to share our concerns and feelings."
3. Play the "name game" in a go-around. Explain that each student will tell his/her name and must also repeat the name of each group member that precedes him/her.
4. Members vote on a group name.

5. Next, each group member tells his/her name and something he/she is good at or likes to do.
6. Explain the concepts of trust and confidentiality. Explain what each is and why each is important. Avoid using the word "secrets."
7. Ask, "What rules will our group need?" Be sure the discussion includes the counselor's concerns such as, raise your hand, wait your turn, no "put downs," arrive on time, etc. Remind them of the #1 rule, confidentiality—explain and discuss its meaning (see *Confidentiality,* page 77).
8. Ask the group members, "What do we mean by listening?" and "Why is listening important?"
9. Play the "Gossip" game.
   a. Divide the group in half.
   b. Explain that you will tell a "Listening Story" (see below) to one of the team members in the hall. Stress that the student cannot ask any questions. The student to whom the story was told will then repeat what he/she heard (again no questions) to another group member. Then, that group member will repeat what he/she heard to another group member. This will continue until everyone on the first team has heard the story. The last person to hear the story will tell aloud what he/she heard. Then you are to read the actual story.
   c. Listening Stories
      Story 1: The storm dropped 15 inches of snow on Washington D.C. Even the weather forecasters were surprised. The next day it seemed strange to see colored leaves peeking out of the snow under a bright blue sky.
      Story 2: Two cats were walking down the road. One saw a squirrel running up a tree and decided to chase it. The squirrel got away, but the cat got stuck in the tree and had to be rescued.
   d. Discuss the importance of listening based on this exercise.
   e. Repeat the activity with the other half of the group using Story 2.

F. Closure:

1. Have each member complete a pre-assessment using the *Evaluation Questions For Communication Group Model* (see page 76). Read them aloud to younger students.
2. Review the group rules and state the time and day of next meeting.
3. Explain the POA (Plan of Action) to be completed before the next session: Have the students ask someone outside of the group to tell them something that happened to him/her. Then they should try to repeat back what was said.

SESSION 2:

A. Objectives:

1. To develop a basic feeling-word vocabulary.
2. To begin to recognize, accept, and share feelings.

B. Materials: Poster board, markers

C. Procedure:

1. Review and discuss the (POA) Plan of Action from Session 1.
2. Ask the students the following questions, "What are feelings?" "Why are feelings important?" "How can you tell how someone is feeling?" Allow time for answers.
3. Then ask, "Has anyone ever played charades?" If necessary, explain the game.
4. Ask for a volunteer to stand and act out (no talking or noise) a feeling word which you whisper to him/her. Tell the group to guess what the feeling is.
5. Repeat until all students have had a chance to act out a feeling.
6. As each feeling is acted out, ask, "When do you feel this way?" Discuss how behavioral clues give hints about feelings. This is important because it enables the group to realize the importance of feelings and understand that people do not readily tell how they feel.
7. Explain that feelings are not good or bad—they just are. What is important is what people do when they feel certain ways.
8. Divide the group into two teams. Use the poster board to record each team's responses.
9. Have one team call out as many pleasant (do not use the word "good") feeling words as possible for one minute. Record the words as they are called out.
10. Repeat the activity with the other team, who will call out unpleasant (do not use the word "bad") feeling words.
11. Tell the group that this list will be used for all the group meetings. If time permits, elicit more feeling words, especially pleasant ones, to add to the list.

D. Closure:

1. Review what feelings are and how feelings are expressed. Stress that feelings are neither good nor bad—what we do with feelings is what matters.
2. Explain the POA (Plan of Action) to be completed before the next session: Observe people between now and the next meeting. Look for situations where you see pleasant feelings and unpleasant feelings. Write or remember at least one. These will be discussed at the next meeting.

SESSION 3:

A. Objectives:

1. Review and develop a feeling-word vocabulary.
2. Understand and apply a "You" message.

B. Materials: *"You" Message* chart (see page 78) for the leader, a copy of *"You" Message* chart for each student, and the list of feeling words from the last session.

C. Procedure:

1. Review and discuss the POA from Session 2.
2. Say: "We have learned that listening is important, and we do what we do because of our feelings, and that all feelings are okay. Today we will learn how to let people know we understand their feelings."

3. Show the *"You" Message* chart.
4. Explain "You" messages in the following manner:
    a. Since others have feelings, a way for you to show you care about others' feelings is to use the following sentence: "You seem ______________." The key is to use a feeling word in the blank.
    b. Use *Scenarios For You Messages* (see page 79) for role playing.
    c. Explain that if the feeling word chosen is not exactly right, the other person will correct it. The important thing is to try to understand by showing another person you are listening.
    d. Have volunteers do step 4b for the group until all have had a chance to practice. Other students should take the leader's place as responders to the volunteer's story.

D. Closure:

1. Review the format and purpose of "You" messages.
2. Give the handout to each student to take home and share with his/her parent(s).
3. Explain the POA (Plan of Action) to be completed before the next session: Write or remember at least one time you used a "You" message.

SESSION 4:

A. Objectives:

1. Review and add to the feeling-word vocabulary.
2. Review a "You" message.
3. Understand and apply an "I" message.

B. Materials: *"I" Message* chart (see page 80) for the leader, a copy of *"I" Message* chart for each student, and the list of feeling words from the second session.

C. Procedure:

1. Review and discuss the POA from Session 3.
2. Show the *"I" Message* chart.
3. Explain "I" messages in the following manner:
    a. Just as others have feelings, and you want to show you care about others' feelings, you also have feelings.
    b. Since all feelings are okay, it is healthy to let others know how you feel about what they do. The important thing is what you do about your feelings.
    c. Refer to the chart on "I" messages. Demonstrate how you give a:
        - complimentary "I" message (+ on the chart).
        - confrontational "I" message (– on the chart).
    d. Note that "I" messages are never to be used as weapons but only as a way to let others know how their behavior affects you.
    e. Demonstrate both types of "I" messages with group members.
    f. Have volunteers practice using "I" messages for the group. Remember: The key is to use a feeling word—Use *Scenarios For I Messages* (see page 81).

D. Closure:

1. Review both types of “I” messages and their purposes.
2. Give each student a copy of the “I” message handout to take home and share with his/her parent(s).
3. Explain the POA (Plan of Action) to be completed before the next session: Write down at least one time before the next session that you used both types of “I” messages.

   Note: The use of each type of message should be reviewed and practiced during the core-content sessions to refine the process so students know when and with whom use is appropriate.

CORE-CONTENT SESSIONS:

It is suggested that the group counseling model include core-content sessions scheduled between the opening and closing sessions. These would be Sessions 2, 3, and 4 in the *Communication Group Model*. If this is not a communication group, you would need to develop the core-content sessions around the students' needs. However, if desired, the model can stand alone as a communication-skills group.

The advantage of a small counseling group goes beyond content, however, because the process is most important. Just the fact that students realize that they are not the only ones experiencing a situation is immensely comforting. This is in addition to the importance students place on what their peers say and think.

Suggested broad areas for small groups are:

- Anger Management (see pages 74-75).
- Self-esteem/Self-concept.
- Divorce adjustment/Blended families.
- Children of alcoholics/Dysfunctional families.
- Study skills, Decision-making/Problem-solving.
- Special needs, e.g., students of deployed military parent(s).

SESSION ( ):

Use this session to follow the core-content sessions. Its number depends on how many sessions were previously conducted.

A. Objectives:

1. To review the skills and understandings learned to date.
2. To differentiate between solvable and unsolvable problems.

B. Materials: A copy of *Worried Walrus* (see page 82) for each student. The leader may want to make a large picture of *Worried Walrus* to show the class.

C. Procedure:

1. Review and discuss the POA from the last session.
2 Ask the group to think of problems they may have. Elicit a problem (of any kind) from each group member. Write each problem on the board.
3. Introduce *Worried Walrus* by showing a picture of him to the group.
4. Explain that there are two things they can do with a problem:
    a. Try their best to find an answer. For example:
        - Study more.
        - Act friendly.
        - Try their best.
    b. Give it to *Worried Walrus* because there is no solution (they can't control the answer). Let him worry for them.
5. Discuss the problems listed on the board and decide whether the student can control or do something about the problem or whether it should be given to *Worried Walrus*. In other words, forget it!
6. Give each student a picture of *Worried Walrus.*
7. In a go-around, have each student (after all have had a chance to think of a problem) turn *Worried Walrus* face down if they can do something to try to solve their problem, or face-up if they are giving it to him because nothing can be done about the problem. Each member must explain his/her choice. What is important is the concept, not a given problem's solution.

D. Closure:

1. Have the students take the *Worried Walrus* handout home and discuss it with their parent(s).
2. Explain the POA (Plan of Action) to be completed before the next session: Write or remember at least two problems before the next group and recall your decision; either to give it to *Worried Walrus* or to do something about it.

SESSION ( ) For ages 9 and older:

A. Objective:

1. To differentiate between rational and irrational thoughts.

B. Materials: A copy of *Worried Walrus* (see page 82) and *Robbie The Robot* (see page 83) for each student.

C. Procedure:

1. Review and discuss the POA for the last session.
2. Ask the students the following question, "Who is responsible for whether you succeed or fail?"
3. Be sure the students understand that individuals determine their own successes or failures, and how they feel about themselves. Individuals also have responsibility for what they do based on the choices they make. Choices are made based on their own feelings about themselves as capable or incapable people.

4. Introduce *Robbie The Robot.* Illustrate the point, through *Robbie The Robot's* negative and positive buttons, that it is the students' choices based on the concepts they have of themselves that make the difference.
5. Give each group member a copy of *Robbie The Robot* and *Worried Walrus.*
6. Review the sheet and ask the students about a time they felt like *Robbie The Robot* when he pushes a negative button.
7. Have volunteers choose a negative button and then find a positive button to push instead. The operative phrase is "We are who we think we are." If we think we are dumb, worthless, a klutz, etc., we will act that way and we will be those things.
8. Introduce *Robbie The Robot* to *Worried Walrus.*
    a. Review what the students learned from *Worried Walrus.* (It is your choice: do something about a problem or give it to *Worried Walrus* to worry for you—forget it!)
    b. Have each group member name any kind of problem. Write these problems on the board.
    c. Have the students turn the *Worried Walrus* and *Robbie The Robot* sheets face down.
9. In a go-around, have each student (after all have had a minute to think of a problem) turn "Robbie" face up if they can do something to solve the problem, or turn "Willie" face-up if they are giving it to him to worry about for them. Each member must explain his/her choice and the other group members are asked whether they agree or not, and why. What is important are the concepts, not a given problem's solution.

D. Closure:

1. Have the students take *Robbie The Robot* home and discuss it with their parent(s).
2. Explain the POA (Plan of Action) to be completed before the next session: Record at least two problems before the next group and recall what your decision was (positive action or give it to *Worried Walrus*).

FINAL SESSION:

A. Objectives:

1. To conclude the group experience in a positive manner.
2. To have each member hear positive comments from the other members.
3. To learn the concept of validation.
4. To have members evaluate the group experience.

B. Materials: A copy of *Positive Words* (see page 84), the *Group Counseling Evaluation* form (see page 86), and the *Evaluation Questions For Communication Group Model* (see page 76); 3 copies of the *Validation Form* (see page 85); 3" X 5" cards equal to the number of students in the group; envelope; and pencil for each student. Copies of the *Validation Form* (see page 85) equal to the number of students in the group for the leader.

C. Procedure:

1. Review and discuss the POA from last session.
2. Elicit feedback from the students by doing the following:
    a. Give each group member the number of 3" X 5" cards equal to the number of students in the group.
    b. Give each member the list of *Positive Words*, an empty envelope, and a pencil.
    c. Explain to the students that: "We have been meeting for a while and since this is our last session, I thought you would like to know how others see you as a person." Remind them that others see them through what they do and how they treat others.
    d. Have each member write his/her name on the envelope and give it to the group leader. He/she then writes his/her name on each 3" x 5" card and gives a card to each member of the group.
    e. Each member then writes one positive word about each person and gives the cards to the leader.
    f. When everyone has completed the cards, the leader puts them in the appropriate envelopes and gives the envelopes back to their owners. Each member then takes turns reading the positive words written about him/her aloud to the group.
    g. Elicit reactions to the experience from the members.
3. Give three blank *Validation Forms* to each group member.
    a. Explain the purpose of sharing your positive feelings to those who are important to you.
    b. Have each member write one validation for someone else and give it to the recipient as soon as possible. Tell the students to use the extra forms whenever they would like to tell someone how they feel.
4. The leader should give a completed *Validation Form* to each member sharing his/her feelings.

D. Closure:

1. Review the main concepts covered in the group.
2. Have the members complete the *Group Counseling Evaluation* form (see page 86). Do this orally with K-2 students. Also, members should complete a post-assessment using the *Evaluation Questions For Group Communication Model* (see page 76). Again, read the ideas aloud to the younger students.

EXAMPLE CORE CONTENT SESSIONS–ANGER MANAGEMENT

Purpose: Students will learn that anger is a normal feeling. Also, they will identify situations that generally provoke anger.

1. Review previous sessions.
2. Read an age-appropriate book on anger management.
3. Inform the students that feeling angry and mad is normal. Ask them to share some other normal feelings.

4. Ask the students to share situations that usually make them feel mad and write these on a chalkboard or chart paper.
5. Have the students write (or draw) the top three things that make them angry.
6. Have them share their answers.
7. Review main points of the session.

Purpose: Students will learn how to recognize signals of when they are feeling angry.

Prior to the lesson, write down feelings (examples—mad, angry, scared, excited, happy, frustrated, worried, proud, and embarrassed) on index cards and place them in a box.

1. Review previous sessions.
2. Say to the students, "Sometimes you can look at a person and tell how he/she is feeling without the person even telling you how he/she feels."
3. Tell the students they are going to play a game. Explain that each of them will draw a feeling card out of the box. Then each child will act out his/her feeling while the other students guess what feeling is being portrayed.
4. Talk about how people may look when they feel angry. (how they may sit, stand, walk, breathe, their facial expressions, clenched fists, gritted teeth, red face, etc.)
5. Give the students crayons or markers and drawing paper and have them draw how they look when they feel angry.
6. Have the students share the pictures.
7. Tell the students to notice when they start to act and look the way they have drawn on their papers because that is a signal they are feeling angry.
8. Review main points of the session.

Purpose: Students will understand that there are appropriate and inappropriate ways of dealing with anger.

Prior to the session, write down various ways of dealing with anger (examples—hitting, talking with a friend, running, yelling at someone, drawing, throwing items, deep breathing, and taking a time-out) on index cards.

1. Review previous sessions.
2. Read an age-appropriate book about feeling angry.
3. Ask the students to tell some of the things the character in the book did when feeling angry.
4. Explain the difference between appropriate ways and inappropriate ways of dealing with anger.
5. Ask the students if they can think of some other things people do when they feel angry. Discuss whether the reactions are appropriate or inappropriate. Write these on the chalkboard or chart paper.
6. Spread the index cards face down on a table. Have the students take turns picking index cards. Have each child decide if it is an appropriate or inappropriate way to respond. Then have each child say what they think the consequence would be if they behaved in the manner that is on the index card he/she chose.
7. Review main points of the session.

EVALUATION QUESTIONS FOR COMMUNICATION GROUP MODEL

(CHECK ONE)

☐ PRE-ASSESSMENT ☐ POST-ASSESSMENT

1. I can list five positive and five negative feeling words.
   ☐ Yes ☐ No

2. I can list the parts of a "You" message.
   ☐ Yes ☐ No

3. I can give an example of a "You" message.
   ☐ Yes ☐ No

4. I can list the parts of an "I" message.
   ☐ Yes ☐ No

5. I can give an example of an "I" message.
   ☐ Yes ☐ No

6. I can explain what a choice is.
   ☐ Yes ☐ No

7. I can explain what a consequence is.
   ☐ Yes ☐ No

8. I can explain my two choices when I have a problem.
   ☐ Yes ☐ No

9. I can show a good way to act when someone teases me.
   ☐ Yes ☐ No

10. I can list five good things about myself.
    ☐ Yes ☐ No

CONFIDENTIALITY

Everything said here remains between us unless you say that:

1. Someone is going to hurt you.
2. You are going to hurt someone else.
3. You are going to hurt yourself.

And then I have to tell someone to keep you safe.

~ Virgena McClanahan

"YOU" MESSAGE

① **Eye contact**

②

______________________________, **you**
NAME

seem ______________________________
FEELING WORD

③

because ______________________________
WHAT YOU OBSERVED

____

____

Example:

"**Ted**, you seem **frustrated** because **you can't find your pencil**."

SCENARIOS FOR "YOU" MESSAGES

"You seem __________ because _________________."

1. A classmate makes fun of your friend. Your friend starts to cry.

2. During a soccer game, your friend scores a goal. He smiles as he walks off the field.

3. Your friend cannot find his homework. He begins pulling everything out of his desk and throwing it on the floor.

4. Your friend wins a school contest. She begins jumping up and down.

5. Your friend gets in trouble in the classroom. She begins to cry.

"I" MESSAGE

____________________, **I feel**
NAME

____
FEELING WORD

when you ____________________
OTHER PERSON'S ACTIONS

____

because ____________________
EFFECT ON YOU

____

Examples:

\+ "**Sally**, I feel **happy** when you **listen to me** because **you are important to me**."

– "**John**, I feel **frustrated** when you **hit me** because **I'm not allowed to hit back**."

SCENARIOS FOR "I" MESSAGES

"I feel _______ when you ___________.
Please do not do it."

1. You are reading out loud to the class, and you mess up. Your friend says, "You are dumb."

2. On the playground, one of your classmates hits you.

3. Your friend takes your homework.

4. One of your friends makes fun of your other friend.

5. One of your classmates grabs a book out of your hand.

6. One of your classmates says you can't be on her team.

WORRIED WALRUS

ROBBIE THE ROBOT

Robbie's head expresses his feelings through his facial expressions. Whether he is happy or sad is determined by the positive or negative statements that he makes about himself and others.

POSITIVE ☺ BUTTONS

SELF

- ☺ If I try, things will be all right.
- ☺ I think I can do it if I try.
- ☺ I am capable of solving my problems.
- ☺ I'll do my best and that's okay.
- ☺ I can make good things happen if I want to.
- ☺ I am a worthwhile person.

OTHERS

- ☺ People usually want to help.
- ☺ People are friendly most of the time.
- ☺ Other people like me.
- ☺ I can usually count on others.
- ☺ People usually care about others.
- ☺ People usually cooperate with me.

NEGATIVE ☹ BUTTONS

SELF

- ☹ I'm no good.
- ☹ I always mess things up.
- ☹ I'm worthless.
- ☹ I'm a klutz.
- ☹ There is nothing I do right.
- ☹ I'm dumb.

OTHERS

- ☹ People are rotten.
- ☹ Everything is other people's fault.
- ☹ Everyone is responsible for my problems.
- ☹ Everybody hates me.
- ☹ People are out to rip me off.
- ☹ I can't trust anybody.

I,______________________________, punch my own buttons.

POSITIVE WORDS

Hardworking	Enthusiastic	Fair
Kind	Handsome	Brave
Likeable	Impressive	Helpful
Lively	Sensitive	Pleasing
Nice	Wonderful	Open-Minded
Polite	Funny	Affectionate
Caring	Courteous	Delightful
Cheerful	Kind-Hearted	Joyous
Exciting	Dependable	Proud
Friendly	Eager	Honest
Happy	Flexible	Enjoyable
Serious	Confident	Sympathetic
Sharing	Glad	Loving
Smart	Beautiful	Responsible
Trusting	Capable	Obedient
Understanding	Competent	Important
Attractive	Ecstatic	Respectful

VALIDATION FORM

SHOWING YOUR FEELINGS FOR SOMEONE ELSE

TO: ____________________

I FEEL ____________________

____

BECAUSE YOU ____________________

____

YOUR NAME____________________

VALIDATION FORM

SHOWING YOUR FEELINGS FOR SOMEONE ELSE

TO: ____________________

I FEEL ____________________

____

BECAUSE YOU ____________________

____

YOUR NAME____________________

GROUP COUNSELING EVALUATION

GROUP NAME

[ ]

MET FOR ________ SESSIONS

1. What did you like about the group meetings?

____

____

____

2. What didn't you like about the group meetings?

____

____

____

3. How could your leader improve the group meetings?

____

____

____

4. What did you learn?

____

____

____

5. How will you use what you learned?

____

____

____

GROUP CONTACT SHEET

Group Meeting Date: ____________ Time: ___________

TEACHER	STUDENT	SESSION 1	SESSION 2	SESSION 3	SESSION 4	SESSION 5	SESSION 6

NOTES

PRE- AND POST-ASSESSMENT EVALUATION RESULTS

GROUP ______________________ DATE __________ TOTAL STUDENT RESPONSES _____

QUESTION NUMBER	1	2	3	4	5	6	7	8	9	10
NUMBER CORRECT PRE-ASSESSMENT										
NUMBER CORRECT POST-ASSESSMENT										
PERCENTAGE OF CHANGE FROM PRE-ASSESSMENT										

CHAPTER 5

THE COUNSELER AS A CONSULTANT

What is consulting?

Consulting is when the important adults in a student's life share information, ideas, and develop strategies to benefit the student.

If consultation is not a direct service to students, how can you justify time to do it?

Actually, consultation is time effective. For example:

- When you help a parent to better deal with his/her child, you are helping a family.
- When you help a teacher, you are helping a classroom of students.

How does counseling compare to consultation?

COUNSELING IS:	CONSULTATION IS:
• Confidential. • A process of direct involvement with a student. • A plan of action developed by the student for the student to act upon.	• Confidential, although it may involve several people with the Child Study Team. • Indirect involvement with a student via the adult consultee. • A plan of action designed and delivered to the student by adult(s) other than the counselor.

What forms can consultation take?

Consultation can be:

- A diagnostic-prescriptive process, as in a Child- or Student Study Team model.
- A staff development model aimed at changing teachers' ways of dealing with students.
- Most typically, a one-on-one interaction with a consultee who wants to make changes or has been referred for changes. For example: a teacher referred by a principal due to lack of classroom control.

What are some consulting do's and don'ts?

Do:

- Use the problem-solving model answered in the question, "How do you systematically help students solve a problem?" (see page 32)
- Keep in mind that the presenting problem may not be the real problem. For example, the frustrated teacher comes for help because he/she can't get students to listen. The real problem is he/she has no classroom-management skills.

- Assess the willingness and ability issues. Take an inventory in your own mind as you assess both issues. Does the person want to change? Is the person able to change?
- Always follow-up and review progress. Provide feedback on what change(s) you can actually observe.
- Follow-through if you are part of the plan. You are then collaborating as well as consulting.
- Cultivate a supportive, friendly, result-oriented image in all you do which will allow for confrontation if needed. For example, a caring listener's feedback counts because you've shown you are there to care, not to criticize.
- Focus on specific behaviors to be changed by the adult consultee.
- Set goals for student change based on behaviors which can be observed. For example, behaviors associated with a negative attitude, not the attitude itself.
- Begin with a reflection of feelings and allow adequate ventilation of feelings even if you don't agree with what is being said.

Don't:

- Come across as an expert. Instead reflect feelings and encourage exploration.
- Ask "why" questions. They cause defensive evasion and rationalization.
- Talk down to the consultees. They must act on their plans and feel they will be able to make changes.
- Seek results at any cost. This may cause the needs of the adult to be served rather than those of the student. For example, the teacher's need for order over the student's need for acceptable movement.

▶ What question do you need to ask yourself when faced with a consultee and his/her problem(s)?

You need to ask yourself if the client's need for change either in him/herself, the student, or both is a question of:

- Willingness to change.
- Ability to change.
- Or both?

For example:

- A parent may be willing to make changes but not have the ability or skills to do so.
- A skilled and able teacher may not be willing to make changes in order to be more effective.
- Your nightmare is when the parent or teacher has neither the willingness nor the ability to change, and wants you to solve the problem. In this case, plan to spend a great deal of time with the consultee.

▶ Why would adults come to you with their problems? Aren't you there to deliver direct services to the students?

Very often the adults are part of the student's problem instead of the solution. By receiving help from the counselor they, in turn, help the student.

For example:

- Parents who set no limits and require no responsible behavior from their children and then can't understand why they won't listen.
- A teacher who does not allow anyone to move without permission cannot understand why a student with Attention Deficit Hyperactive Disability (ADHD) is having trouble following the rules.

▶ What is one approach to use when helping teachers or parents change a student's behavior?

Have the adult consultee use the *Behavior Frequency Assessment Chart* (see page 95). List the behaviors desired and rate them as to their frequency. Rate this behavior at the beginning, during, and after the agreed-upon time to try interventions.

▶ How does the *Behavior Frequency Assessment Chart* work?

In the sample chart, Becky has improved on all behaviors targeted for intervention by the teacher after a period of four weeks.

BEHAVIOR FREQUENCY ASSESSMENT CHART

STUDENT **Becky** TEACHER **Burns** GRADE **5**

LENGTH OF ASSESSMENT TIME **4 Weeks** **Nov. 5th-Nov. 30th**

List the student's behaviors. Check the frequency of each behavior listed. You may make additional comments.

DESIRED BEHAVIORS	VERY SELDOM			SELDOM			SOMETIMES			OFTEN			VERY OFTEN		
	PRE	DURING	POST	PRE	DURING	POST	PRE	DURING	POST	PRE	DURING	POST	PRE	DURING	POST
Completes Assignments	✔				✔				✔						
Follows Directions	✔				✔				✔						
Stays In Seat	✔							✔				✔			
Raises Hand Before Speaking	✔							✔				✔			
Argues With Teacher									✔		✔		✔		

Does this mean that Becky's problem no longer exists?

- No, because you don't have a magic wand. However, this approach stresses two things:
    1. The goal of improvement.
    2. The idea that change is a process of gradual improvement and the teacher can reinforce change.

The key is leading the adult consultee to pair what he/she needs to change with the desired behavior change in the student(s).

- This means that the operative questions for the consultee are:
    - "What would I like to see happen?"
    - "What do I need to change to make it happen?"

What is the Child Study Team approach?

The Child Study Team is a group of professionals usually including the referring teacher, a designee or the principal, the counselor, and a specialist such as a psychologist or a social worker who meet to:

- Collect information.
- Brainstorm ideas and possible strategies.
- Develop a Plan of Action.
- Assign a case manager.
- Assign responsibilities.
- Track interventions.

What is the process of the Child Study Team (CST)?

The process of a CST has three levels of activity:

- Level A—Pre-referral
    - This is what is done before a formal referral. If this works, a formal referral is not needed.
- Level B—Referral to the team
    - The team develops a Plan of Action (POA).
- Level C—Referral for full evaluation
    - This level is reached if the pre-referral and the team's POA still have not produced the desired change(s).
    - The student is evaluated for possible handicapping conditions.
    - This involves parental rights, timelines, and legal considerations.

It is important to remember that the purpose of the CST is:

- To gather information and track interventions within regular education.
- Not to screen or test for special education placement.

The *Child Study Team Chart* (see page 96) summarizes the CST process.

What are some other ways to consult with adults?

Conduct staff development programs.

- Teach parents and teachers basic communication skills (see Chapter 2).
- In a follow-up workshop, teach parents and teachers the problem-solving process.
  - Divide the group into triads. Have one person be the speaker, another the listener, and the third the observer.
  - Have the speaker give three or four sentences about a topic that reflects a problem.
  - The listener should take the speaker through the problem-solving process (see pages 32-33).
  - The observer should note the skills observed and give feedback on what was seen and heard.
  - Rotate the roles until each person has had a chance to be a speaker, a listener, and an observer.

Conduct parent training/support groups.

Give PTA presentations and community workshops. These are discussed more fully in Chapter 10.

Consultation does not always have to be counselor-initiated. Encourage teachers to meet, preferably in triads, on a regular basis to discuss with other teachers open-ended concerns they have.

Summary:

You will be successful as a consultant if you remember to:

- Focus on and reinforce specific target behaviors in both your consultee and his/her student.
- Realize that changing one's behavior is threatening and risky no matter how much it may be needed. To be successful you must reinforce and encourage small improvements, not quick-fixes.
- Lay the groundwork for success as a consultant every day with the behavior you model. Be a caring, non-judgmental listener whom others will seek for help.

BEHAVIOR FREQUENCY ASSESSMENT CHART

STUDENT ______________________ TEACHER ______________________ GRADE ______

LENGTH OF ASSESSMENT TIME ______________________ __________ – __________

List the student's behaviors. Check the frequency of each behavior listed. You may make additional comments.

DESIRED BEHAVIORS	VERY SELDOM			SELDOM			SOMETIMES			OFTEN			VERY OFTEN		
	PRE	DURING	POST	PRE	DURING	POST	PRE	DURING	POST	PRE	DURING	POST	PRE	DURING	POST

*Adapted from R. D. Myrick

CHILD STUDY TEAM CHART

*Adapted from L. Cribbs

A	B	C
↓	↓	↓
STEP 1 Teacher identifies the problem(s).	**STEP 1** Teacher makes a formal request for assistance to the Child Study Team.	**STEP 1** CST refers student for consideration of handicapping condition. Referral is completed at CST meeting.
↓	↓	↓
STEP 2 Teacher contacts the parent(s). Teacher should document the contact with the date, time, subject, and relevant comments.	**STEP 2** Teacher participates in Child Study Team (CST) meeting with other members: Counselor Social Worker Principal Psychologist	**STEP 2** Full evaluation done with student including: Psychological Social history Medical Educational Hearing screening Observation
↓	↓	↓
STEP 3 Teacher discusses problem with principal, counselor, and/or resource teacher to develop interventions.	**STEP 3** CST develops a plan of strategies to be tried by teachers and others. Plan should be documented.	**STEP 3** Meeting is set up to discuss evaluation results and eligibility for special placement due to handicapping condition.
↓	↓	↓
STEP 4 Teacher tries interventions: Counseling Parent contact(s) Resource help Reduced workload Modified instruction (If problem is not resolved, go to Level B.	**STEP 4** CST reviews plan to decide if it needs to be modified, is successful, or if the problem needs to go to Level C. Level C only takes place if recommended by CST.	**STEP 4** (If found eligible) IEP meeting with: Teacher Psychologist Principal Social Worker Counselor Special Ed. Rep Parents

CHAPTER 6

GROUP GUIDANCE

What is group guidance?

Group guidance is:

- Planned, sequential, interrelated units of information designed to meet the developmental needs of all students in the school.
- The main prevention area of the guidance program.
- Presented in units to groups of 10 students or more.
- Units that are designed to meet specific objectives.
- One of the two direct services the counselor delivers to students, counseling being the other.

Is the guidance and counseling program a separate curriculum?

No. It is important to remember that the total guidance and counseling program is a program of services—not a separate curriculum.

What is the main difference between group guidance and counseling?

Group guidance is basically the sharing and teaching of information and skills.

Counseling is a confidential process of direct intervention activities designed to change behavior, delivered by a qualified school counselor.

Both involve learning and changing behavior; the difference lies in the:

- Number of students.
- Type of interaction possible.
- Qualifications of the leader.

What are the positive and negative aspects of group guidance?

The positive aspects of group guidance are that it:

- Is an efficient use of the counselor's time.
- Is an effective means to systematically teach skills and understanding to all students and to reach special-needs groups.
- Defines the counselor and what he/she can do for students and teachers as a:
    - Skilled, friendly adult.
    - Visible, inviting helper.
    - Model for teachers on how to deliver affective lessons.
- Can allow teachers, with encouragement, administrative support, and counselor help, to teach the lessons in the classroom guidance program and thereby free the counselor for special-needs group guidance and all the other things the counselor must do.

The negative aspects of group guidance are that it:

- Can become time-consuming and overwhelming if the counselor is scheduled regularly as part of a "master schedule."
- Can become a "dog and pony" show if the classroom program is fragmented and is there mainly to give the teacher a "break."

How are group guidance units typically organized?

Group guidance units are typically organized by developmental and grade levels as classroom guidance programs.

Group guidance units should be infused and correlated into the regular academic curriculum wherever possible.

- Learning to cooperate can be part of group projects in social studies.
- Writing stories on a variety of affective topics can be part of language arts.
- Drawing pictures associated with feelings can be part of an art class.
- Cooperatively solving problems in math or in current events classes can help students learn to get along with each other and respect the opinions of others.

Group guidance can also address the special needs of students, such as latchkey students, death affecting the whole school, cliques, perfectionism, etc.

- A unit on "Mistakes" can help students accept and learn from their mistakes rather than be critical of themselves for lacking perfection.
- A unit on "Cliques" can help prevent hurt feelings and unkind treatment of fellow students.
- Latchkey students can discuss their responsibilities when home alone and their feelings about their situations.

State and local requirements such as student competencies in problem-solving skills, decision-making, etc., also affect the type of units presented.

What is a developmental classroom guidance program?

Just as students develop physically and cognitively, so they develop socially and emotionally.

A developmental guidance program is a series of lessons that matches the needs and the developmental ages of the students. (see *Developmental Ages Chart*, pages 107-108).

Development is continuous but uneven, while grade levels are arbitrary placements based on age. The *Developmental Ages Chart* (adapted from Muro and Dinkmeyer, Counseling in the Elementary and Middle School: A Pragmatic Approach, 1977, see pages 107-108) relates skills and understandings in the affective realm to chronological ages of students. Development should be viewed as a continuous sequence of skills and understanding to be mastered. All previous learning is deepened and expanded at the next level.

How is it possible to approach the task of teaching classroom guidance?

There are basically two ways to teach a classroom guidance program.

- The first is when the counselor teaches all the lessons with no teacher follow-up.
- The second is when the counselor teaches some lessons which are correlated to the school curriculum, and the teachers teach part of the program and follow-up on the counselor's efforts.

What do you want parents and teachers to understand about classroom guidance?

Parents and teachers should understand that their students are learning about:

- Their own unique selves.
- Their own unique feelings.
- The feelings of others.
- How feelings relate to behavior.
- The decision-making process.
- How responsibility means accepting the consequences of one's actions.
- How to solve problems with others.
- The world of work and how it relates to their future role as workers.

What are some ways you can teach the introductory lesson?

In grades Kindergarten through second you can:

- Divide poster board into four parts. On each part draw a face showing a different basic feeling—happy, sad, angry, afraid.
- Then, in the classroom, have the students relate a time when they have had each feeling and, if time permits, draw a picture of one situation.

In grades three through six you can:

- Divide a poster board in fourths. Find pictures illustrating four basic feelings and glue them to the poster board.
- Divide another poster board in half for situation cards. Find or draw two situations where one of the people pictured had to make a decision. An example of a decision-making picture would be a picture showing a boy who has broken a window and is running away, and another boy who is watching the incident.
- In the classroom, share the four feeling pictures and ask students to share a time when they have had similar feelings.
- Then, share the situation cards and have students answer the following questions:
  - "How would you feel if this were you?"
  - "What is one thing you could do to solve the problem?"
- Give each student a *There is a Counselor in Your Elementary School* brochure (see page 109) or one like it to take home and share with his/her parents.

- Tell the students where you are located in the school and when you will be coming to their classroom.
- Ask them if they know what a counselor does. Elicit from them that your job is to help if there is anything bothering them that could interfere with their learning. They should also know that you and their teacher will work together to help them.

How do you organize and deliver classroom guidance programs?

The unit is the preferred service delivery model. The unit is a systematic, coordinated series of lessons designed to address the needs of students at each grade level.

What is the unit concept?

A unit entails a focused sequential approach to a topic. For example, a series of lessons (minimum of four, maximum of six) delivered in a defined time frame, such as, twice a week for two weeks during a particular month. (See Chapter 8 for scheduling ideas.)

Materials are so numerous and have improved so much in the past 20 years that no attempt to provide specifics will be made here. Rather, general suggestions will be made since the number of lessons taught will vary with your purpose and demands upon your time, as well as your students' needs. It is suggested that counselors carefully review different programs and adopt those that are suitable for their needs.

What is the format for classroom guidance lessons?

Generally, 30-minute lessons are easier to schedule and long enough to teach a concept. However, 30 minutes is rarely long enough to have students write much.

One suggestion is to make a presentation for 15 minutes and allow 15 minutes for an activity, processing, demonstration, and a check for understanding.

- In the last 15 minutes, you can have the students participate in an accompanying activity such as illustrating a picture which, if possible, includes themselves.

Students like to keep any drawings or papers that they do and therefore it is suggested that each student keep a folder with an appropriate title, such as "All About Me." When the unit is completed, the students can take their folders home along with a cover sheet from you explaining what they have studied . (For the sample letter for kindergarten, see page 110 and for the letters for all other grades, see pages 111-112.)

Since feelings are the basis of all actions, it is appropriate to do the same opening lesson focusing on feelings and the procedures, methods, and rules used in each grade level from first through sixth.

What is an appropriate classroom guidance approach for Kindergarten?

In Kindergarten, the focus is mainly on feelings and a positive self-concept.

Activities appropriate to this age are the development of feeling words—happy, sad, mad and glad, and to participate in positive self-esteem activities. For example:

- The leader (counselor or teacher) can ask questions such as:
  "How do you feel when …
  - someone gives you a present?"
  - a pet dies?"
  - a friend moves away?"

Students do not draw well at this age, so songs, videos, or simple role-plays with you, others, or puppets can increase understanding.

A follow-up lesson might involve the leader or students pantomiming a decision situation and the class guessing the feeling. Stress that feelings are neither right nor wrong—they just are.

Another activity is to have the students "draw" faces on a chalkboard and tell when they felt this way or make faces and have others guess what feelings their expressions portray.

See page 113 for a K-2 lesson on a common problem: tattling.

What is an appropriate classroom guidance approach for first grade?

The main focus in first grade is on the self and the concept that feelings are "okay."

Continue with role-playing and pantomiming of feelings.

Add to the feeling words learned in Kindergarten. Make a chart with the students.

Self-concept activities which give everyone a turn in the "spot light" are appropriate. For example:

- "I'm thinking of a girl who has red hair and likes to share her toys. Who is she?"

Play different kinds of music and ask how it makes them feel.

Puppets are especially well-received at this age and can be used to role-play situations related to feelings and self-esteem.

The concept of mistakes is a good topic to focus on. Use the idea that everyone makes mistakes—a mistake does not make someone a bad person. What is important is what is learned to help prevent it from happening again.

What is an appropriate classroom approach for second grade?

The important focus in the second grade is on the relationship of one's self to others and on responsible behavior.

Use activities showing feelings, and process what can be done when others are unkind and feelings are hurt.

Common problems, such as sharing, taking turns, and making fun of others can be explored through role-playing.

Drawings can be made that show what can be done when someone is left out.

Discussions are also appropriate.

What is an appropriate classroom guidance approach for third grade?

This is a good age to emphasize that feelings are related to actions.

Develop the concept that trust is related to responsibility. We trust those who demonstrate responsible behaviors. We can count on them to make responsible choices. The following approach is adaptable and can serve as content for grades 4-6 as well.

Teach the students the following questions to consider when they have a choice to make:
1. How do you feel? (About the situation) 2. What could you do? (Alternative choices) 3. What might happen? (Possible consequences)

A good way to teach students about choices and consequences is have the students generate a list of problem situations encountered at home and in school.

- Students can begin generating choices for problem-solving, then tie alternative choices to possible consequences using the above three questions.
- If desired, you can purchase situation cards or make your own by pasting pictures from magazines on pieces of cardboard showing problem situations. You will find many students jump from feelings to immediate action, and do not consider the consequences. For example, Joe calls Bill a name, so Bill hits Joe.

A culminating activity might be a centrally located problem-solving bulletin board with situations drawn and written out. For example:

THIRD GRADE LEARNS TO MAKE GOOD CHOICES		
(Description of Problem) **SOMEONE COPYING FROM YOUR PAPER**		
CHOICE 1 **Cover your paper**	CHOICE 2 **Move your seat**	CHOICE 3 **Tell him/her to stop**

What is an appropriate classroom guidance approach for fourth grade?

Feelings and choices can be deepened, as well as tied to a communication activity at this age.

You may adapt the skills and activities from the *Communication Group Model* (see pages 66-75, reproducible forms/worksheets for the sample model on pages 76-86), emphasizing listening behaviors, the concept of empathy, and "You" and "I" messages.

See sample lessons for Grades 4-6 on respect and listening (see pages 114-116), a peaceful environment (see pages 117-118), and following directions (including a pre- and post-test, see pages 119-125).

What is an appropriate classroom guidance approach for fifth and sixth grades?

Activities for grades five and six have much overlap.

The communication group activities for grade four would also be appropriate for grade five.

- Review "What is a careful listener?" as an appropriate way to begin the unit.

This age should also be involved in group activities and group problem-solving.

- One activity which is very popular is the *Positive T-Shirt.* Have the group name positive quality/characteristic words and write them on the board. Divide the class into groups of five or six. Have each group member write a positive characteristic or word about every other group member on a sticky label. Give each group member a copy of the *Positive T-Shirt* (see page 126). As each member's *Positive T-Shirt.* is passed around, the group members should stick their positive comment on it. If desired, the group members could bring in real T-shirts and group members could write their comments directly on the T-shirts.

Next, the students can be taught to process situations and come to a group consensus on solving problems.

- Divide the students into groups and select a leader for each group.
- Give each group a copy of *Problem-Solving* (see page 127) for each problem to be solved.
- Give each group a number and each problem to be solved a number. These numbers should be written on the *Problem-Solving* sheet.
- Assign a problem to each group. It should be a three or four sentence situation which has been generated either by the leader or the students.
- Set a time limit for the group to come to a consensus. Each group should begin to solve the problem given and write its solution on the *Problem-Solving* sheet.
- Each group leader should report to the class what the group members' solution was to their situation, and how they worked together to make that choice.

Remember that the quality of the decision is secondary to the problem-solving process.

What are some counselor behaviors for effective classroom management?

Learn and intentionally model the following communication skills as outlined in Chapter 2.

- Non-judgmental listening.
- Questioning.
- Use of restatements.
- Use of feeling statements.

If you call upon a student who has his/her hand raised and he/she cannot respond, say, "We'll come back to you later."

Acknowledge contributions whether they are exactly correct or not. For example, say, "Thanks" or "Thanks for sharing."

Use proximity control and movement both to maintain control and heighten student interest.

Use a circular or semicircular group arrangement whenever possible. When everyone can see everyone else, it encourages open communication.

Most importantly, set a few rules and consequences for breaking the rules, such as:

- "One person speaks at a time." This is the one rule you really need.
- The three-strike rule works to set limits and sends a message to those talking inappropriately (see page 128).
    - When a repeat offender gets to two strikes, often he/she will comply.
    - If not, after three strikes the offender should be removed from the group, either in or out of the room.
    - Do this by simply saying, "I'm sorry _______, but you don't seem to be able to follow the rules today, so you can't take part in the class. We'll try again next time."

How do you evaluate your classroom guidance program?

Ideally student developmental needs in the social, personal, and emotional areas have been correlated with and infused into the existing academic curriculum.

Evaluation procedures should be stipulated along with expected behaviors when the unit is designed.

A valid evaluation is the observed performance of students by their teacher as they use the skills and demonstrate understanding on the material covered in the unit.

Student and teacher evaluations (see pages 129-130) measure both behavior and understanding of content. Student evaluations should be completed during the last lesson of the unit. At completion of the unit, the counselor should discuss teacher follow-up of the unit. Give the evaluation form to the teacher two to four weeks after the completion of unit.

What are some ways to follow-through and inform parents about what happened in their child's classroom guidance program?

In addition to the student evaluation, collect the booklets each student has kept during the classroom guidance unit after the students put them in order. After reading them, return them to the students to take home. The students like taking the booklets home and the parents have the opportunity to review with them the main ideas they learned.

Staple a short letter to parents on the top of the booklets (for sample letters, see pages 110-112).

This is good public relations and helps keep parents informed and interested.

What about the "special needs" topics that often need to be addressed in schools?

The following are examples of the types of groups that would be addressed on an "as needed" basis:

- Dealing with a student's death and how it affects students.
- Problems on a school bus.
- Rules and responsibilities in a classroom.
- Dealing with negative peer pressure.
- Study skills.

How do I schedule all these classroom guidance programs?

For scheduling ideas, see Chapter 8, page 156, as well as previous remarks. in this chapter.

What about teaching conflict resolution?

A very effective means of teaching students to deal with conflicts is shown on pages 131-132. The counselor can train teachers to work with/monitor this process in their classrooms.

Summary:

Group guidance is an efficient and effective way to deal with student groups of 10 or more whose needs can be addressed through teaching specific skills and understandings.

Group guidance works best when its content is infused into the regular academic curriculum and delivered in combination by the teachers and the counselor.

The counselor should not be scheduled into a master plan since continuity and focus are lost. When coupled with encroaching coordination duties, little time will be left for counseling.

DEVELOPMENTAL AGES CHART

Grade K-1

THE FIVE-YEAR-OLD CHILD

Is "good," helpful, conforming
Attempts only those things ensuring success
Needs attention, affection, praise
Is energetic and "fidgety"
Has short attention span
May show opposite extremes of behavior
"Good" behavior may break up as the school year progresses

THE SIX-YEAR-OLD CHILD

Is extremely egocentric; wants to be the center of attention, "best" and "first"
Has boundless energy
May be oppositional, silly, brash, critical
Cries easily; shows a variety of tension-releasing behaviors
Is attached to the teacher
Has difficulty being flexible
Often considers fantasy real

GOAL:
Understanding self

OBJECTIVES:
- Positive, realistic self-concept
- Respect for self
- One's own uniqueness
- Awareness of feelings
- Expression of feelings
- Group participation
- Learning from mistakes

Grade 2

THE SEVEN-YEAR-OLD CHILD

Behavior is more calm
Can begin to reason and concentrate
Worries, is self-critical, and expresses lack of confidence
Demands teacher's time
Dislikes being singled out, even for praise

GOAL:
Understanding self and others

OBJECTIVES:
- Self-concept
- Understanding others
- Respect for others
- Relationship with others
- Responsibility

Grade 3

THE EIGHT-YEAR-OLD CHILD

Is explosive, excitable, dramatic, inquisitive
Possesses "know-it-all" attitude
Is able to assume more responsibility for actions
Actively seeks praise
May undertake more than can be handled successfully
Is self-critical
Recognizes needs of others

GOAL:
Understanding goals, behavior, self

OBJECTIVES:
- Relationship of feelings, goals, and behavior
- Choices and consequences
- Setting goals
- Responsibility
- Working with others

Grade 4

THE NINE-YEAR-OLD CHILD

Is an age of "general confusion"
Wants distance between child and adults;
may rebel against authority
Needs group membership
Seeks independence
Possesses high activity level
Can express wide range of emotions and verbalize easily
Can empathize
Can think independently and critically, but tied to peer standards
Begins to increase sense of truthfulness
Is typically not self-confident

GOAL:
Choices and decisions

OBJECTIVES:

- Decision-making process
- Greater responsibility
- Personal standards
- Personal interests and abilities
- Social skills
- Group decision-making

Grade 5

THE TEN-YEAR-OLD CHILD

Has positive approach to life
Tends to be obedient, good-natured, and fun
Possesses surprising scope of interests
Finds TV is very important; identifies with TV characters
Is capable of increasing independence
Shows increase of truthfulness, dependability
Tends to improve self-concept and acceptance of others
Forms good personal relationships with teachers and counselors

GOAL:
Communication skills and
the changing self

OBJECTIVES:

- Listening and responding
- Problem-solving
- Maturational changes
- Peer and adult expectations

Grade 6

THE ELEVEN-YEAR-OLD CHILD

Heads towards adolescence
Shows more self-assertion, curiosity
Has social expansiveness and awareness
Has physical exuberance, is restless, wiggly, talks a lot
Has range and intensity of emotionality, moody, easily frustrated
Can relate feelings
Is competitive, wants to excel, may put down "out group"
Has "off-color" humor, silliness
Teases and tussles

THE TWELVE-YEAR-OLD CHILD

Enters the stage in-between childish and mature behavior
Is spirited, enthusiastic
Can "stay put" longer; exercises self-control
Has growing sense of intuition and insight into self and others
Is less moody; may be good-natured around adults
Becomes increasingly self-reliant and self-centered
Is curious but not ready for long-term planning
Has strong desire to be like peers

GOAL:
The changing self
and increased independence

OBJECTIVES:

- Coping with changes
- Transition to adolescence
- Interpersonal skills
- Peer groups/pressure
- Personal interests and abilities
- Greater responsibility for behavior and decisions

THERE IS A COUNSELOR IN YOUR ELEMENTARY SCHOOL

The counselor works with students in the classroom.

The counselor works with students in small groups.

The counselor works with students individually.

The counselor and teachers work together to help children.

The counselor works with parents.

The counselor works with school resource personnel and community agencies.

Dear Parents,

Please call (_____) ________________________
if you have more questions or a concern.

Guidance services are for everyone.

Dear Parents,

Recently, your child has been involved in classroom guidance activities. In these classes, developmental concepts related to responsibility and one's own unique qualities were taught.

Specifically we studied:

Feelings—How feelings help make us special, and that everyone has feelings.

Responsibility—What responsibility is, and that others count on you to do your best.

We also studied the concepts of: sharing, taking turns, working together, taking care of property, and caring about others' feelings.

Each child completed the booklet *All About Me*. Please take time to share your child's booklet and to reinforce the idea that he/she is a **V**ery **I**mportant **P**erson.

Please feel free to call if you have any questions or comments.

____
SCHOOL COUNSELOR

Dear Parents,

Recently, your child has been involved in classroom guidance activities. In these classes, developmental concepts related to responsibility and to problem-solving were taught.

Specifically we studied:

Feelings—Identified feelings and discussed how feelings relate to one's choices.

Responsibility—Learned what it is and that a responsible person accepts the consequences of his/her own actions.

Trust—Discovered why responsible people are trusted.

Choices—Realized how a person's feelings about problems can block his/her problem-solving choices. Responsible choices contain three parts—How does a person feel? What can be done? What might happen?

Alternatives—Learned to generate many possible ways to solve a problem.

Predicting—Explored what might happen when different alternatives are tried.

Consequences—Recognized what the outcomes of one's actions might be.

During the classes, each child completed an *All About Me* booklet. Please take time to share your child's booklet and to reinforce the idea that he/she is a **V**ery **I**mportant **P**erson.

Please feel free to call if you have any questions or comments.

____

SCHOOL COUNSELOR

Dear Parents,

I have recently conducted classroom guidance activities with your child and all the students at his/her grade level.

In the fourth and fifth grades, I focused on teaching communication skills.

Students were taught:

- To identify their own feelings.
- Ways their actions affect others' feelings.
- Ways to share their feelings with others.
- To identify feeling words to use.
- To listen carefully.
- To listen with empathy (putting yourself in another's shoes).
- The four steps to being a helpful listener:
    1. Paying attention.
    2. Listening for the words and ideas.
    3. Listening with your heart (empathy).
    4. Saying something to show you care (using a feeling word).
- How to generate alternatives to deal with conflicts and avoid conflicts.
- How to think what might happen (the consequences of actions) based on the choices they could make.

Each child completed an *All About Me* booklet. Please take time to share your child's booklet and to reinforce the idea that he/she is a **V**ery **I**mportant **P**erson.

Please feel free to call if you have any questions or comments.

____
SCHOOL COUNSELOR

TATTLING

Kindergarten-Grade 2

Purpose:

To teach students when it is appropriate to tell the teacher and when it is considered tattling

Materials:

- ☐ Age-appropriate book on tattling
- ☐ *Stop* sign and *Go* sign
- ☐ Tape
- ☐ Scenarios of incidents that initiate tattling or telling

  Example scenarios:
    Someone cuts in line
    Someone is throwing rocks on the playground
    Someone is not doing his/her work
    Someone is hitting you

Procedure:

Read the selected storybook.

Ask the students pertinent questions relating to the story such as why others were angry at the main character, would you want to be friends with someone who acted like this, and when should you tell on someone to the teacher.

Explain to the students the appropriate times to tell the teacher. Let them know it isn't tattling when the person is hurting him/herself, another student, or you, or destroying property. Under these circumstances, telling an adult is the right thing to do.

Inform the students that everyone is going to play a game. Post the *Go* sign on one side of the room and the *Stop* sign on the other side of the room. Tell the students you are going to read some scenarios. Instruct them to walk to the *Go* sign if it is a time when they should tell their teacher and to walk to the *Stop* sign if it is a time they should not tattle.

Read the scenarios.

Conclusion: Remind the students that the only time they should tell the teacher is when someone is hurting him/herself, another student, or hurting you or destroying property. All other times they should ignore the other person or work it out on their own.

RESPECT
Grades 4-6

Purpose:

To teach students the meaning of respect, to respect differences, identify people they respect, and to understand the importance of *The Golden Rule*

Materials:

- ☐ *Listen Carefully* (page 115) for the leader
- ☐ *People I Show Respect* (page 116) for the leader
- ☐ Chalkboard and chalk
- ☐ Paper and pencil or markers for each student

Procedure:

Explain to students that the lesson will focus on respect.

Review the classroom rules.

Define respect. Include an explanation of *The Golden Rule.*

Play *Listen Carefully.* Point out similarities and differences. Discuss how people have to respect others' differences.

Read the statements on *People I Show Respect*. Have the class guess who you are talking about. Write responses on the chalkboard. Have the students provide one example of how they can show each person respect.

Distribute a piece of paper and a pencil or markers to each student. Have the students draw a picture of someone they respect, then share their completed drawing with the group/class.

Summarize the lesson. Include *The Golden Rule.*

LISTEN CAREFULLY

Tell the students to listen carefully to what you are about to say, then follow your directions.

Stand up if you are in (GRADE TO WHOM YOU ARE PRESENTING) grade.

Raise your right arm if you have a brother.

Stand on one foot if you like to play sports.

Clap your hands twice if you have brown hair.

Pat your head if your favorite school subject is math.

Place your hands on your knees if you are an only child.

Hop two times if you like to dance.

Take one step back if you are (AGE OF MOST STUDENTS) years old.

Rub your tummy if you are feeling happy right now.

Sit back down in your seat if you are in (NAME OF TEACHER)'s class.

PEOPLE I SHOW RESPECT

I teach you how to keep your body in shape, and we play fun games when you come to see me.

I safely drive students to and from school in a yellow bus.

I wear a badge and help keep the community safe.

I serve food to students during lunch time.

I am in this classroom with you all week teaching you all sorts of exciting information.

From the time you were born, I have been taking care of you. I love you very much.

I drive a big, red truck, and I put out fires.

I teach you all about art.

I am the boss of the school, and I help students solve problems.

I teach you how to sing beautifully.

I am your parents' parents, and I am very grand.

I keep this school sparkling clean.

I let students check out my books.

I am in the classroom with you, and I may even sit by you.

PROMOTING A PEACEFUL ENVIRONMENT

Grades 4-6

Purpose:

To teach students behaviors that will promote peaceful living

Materials:

- ☐ *Promoting A Peaceful Environment* (page 118) for each student
- ☐ Pencil for each student

Procedure:

Discuss the meaning of the word *peace* and how it is evidenced in everyday living.

Have the students compare their answers to everyday living that is not peaceful.

Give each student a copy of *Promoting A Peaceful Environment.* Have the students complete the activity sheet, then discuss their answers.

PROMOTING A PEACEFUL ENVIRONMENT

1. Avoid saying words that are ______________________________ to others.

2. Treat others with ____.

3. Everyone sees every situation the same way.
   ☐ True ☐ False

4. When in a small group, you should ___________________________ with your team.

5. A *put up* is a *compliment*. Give an example of a put up. ______________________
   ____

6. When working in groups, it is important for one person to make all the decisions.
   ☐ True ☐ False

7. What is a positive thing that happens when using put-ups? ___________________
   ____

8. What is a negative thing that happens when using put-downs? ________________
   ____

9. Put downs are a healthy way to communicate.
   ☐ True ☐ False

10. A frown and thumbs-down are examples of _________________________________.

11. A smile, nod, and thumbs-up are all _____________________________________.

12. Promote ______________________________ in the classroom.

13. It is okay to disagree with one of your friends?
    ☐ True ☐ False

14. Getting to know each other will promote a peaceful environment.
    ☐ True ☐ False

15. Name one type of compliment. ____

FOLLOWING DIRECTIONS

Grades 4-6

Purpose:

Students will learn about following directions and why following directions is important.

Materials:

- ☐ *Following Directions: Student Pre-Test* (page 121) for each student
- ☐ *Following Directions Activity Sheet* (page 122) for each student
- ☐ *Following Directions: Student Post-Test* (page 123) for each student
- ☐ Pencil for each student
- ☐ *Following Directions: Teacher Survey* (page 124) for each teacher
- ☐ *Following Directions Poster* (page 125) for each classroom

Procedure:

Introduce yourself and review classroom rules.

Give each student a copy of the *Following Directions: Student Pre-Test* and a pencil. Inform the students that you are not grading the pre-test, so they do not need to worry if they are unsure of the answers. Have the students complete the pre-test, then collect them.

Play *Simon Says* for approximately 10-15 commands. Then ask the students what they needed to do in order to play *Simon Says*. Acknowledge all the students' responses. If the students do not come up with the correct answer, let them know they had to follow directions in order to do well at *Simon Says*.

Inform the students that today's lesson focuses on following directions.

Ask the students the *who, what's, when, where, why*, and *how* of following directions:

Who: Ask the students, "Who has to follow directions?"

What: Ask the students, "What does following directions mean?" and "What are two types of directions you have to follow in school?" (verbal and written)

When: Ask the students, "When do you have to follow directions in school?"

Where: Ask the students, "Where else do you have to follow directions?"

Why: Ask the students, "Why do you have to follow directions?"

How: Ask the students, "How do you look when you are following directions?" (Make sure the students answer this question in regards to both verbal and written directions.)

Give each student a copy of *Following Directions.* Have the students individually complete the activity sheet. Then ask the following questions.

Who figured out the trick of this worksheet?

What was the trick?

Explain to the students why it was important to follow the directions on the worksheet.

Closure:

Review the key points of the lesson. Ask the students the following questions:

Who has to follow directions?

What does following directions mean?

What are the two types of directions you have to follow at school?

When do you have to follow directions?

Where do you follow directions?

How do you look when you are following directions?

Why do you have to follow directions?

Give each student a copy of the *Following Directions: Student Post-Test*. Have the students complete the post-test, then collect them.

Post a copy of the *Following Directions Sign* in each classroom.

Evaluation:

Compare the students' pre- and post-tests. Share the results with the classroom teachers.

Give the teachers the *Following Directions: Teacher's Survey* to complete and return to you.

FOLLOWING DIRECTIONS

STUDENT PRE-TEST

Name ________________________________ Date: ______________

Directions: Answer the questions the best that you can.

1. Who has to follow directions?

____

____

2. What does *following directions* mean?

____

____

3. What are two types of directions you have to follow at school?

____

____

4. How does someone look when following directions?

____

____

5. Why is it important to follow directions?

____

____

FOLLOWING DIRECTIONS

Date: ____________

Name ______________________________

1. Read carefully all of the following directions before doing anything.
2. Write your name on the top line.
3. Circle the first word in number 2.
4. Underline the last word in number 2.
5. Quickly draw a small picture of yourself beside your name.
6. Draw a triangle next to the number 5.
7. On the line below, write what you are learning about in math.

   ____

8. On the line below, write what your favorite thing is to eat at lunch.

   ____

9. Draw a square around the even numbers.
10. Draw a circle around the odd numbers.
11. On the blank, write what 5 multiplied by 4 equals: ____________
12. Now that you have read all the directions, only do numbers 2 and 5.

FOLLOWING DIRECTIONS

STUDENT POST-TEST

Name ______________________________ Date: ____________

Directions: Answer the questions the best that you can.

1. Who has to follow directions? ______________________________

   ____

2. What does *following directions* mean? ______________________________

   ____

3. What are two types of directions you have to follow at school?

   ____

   ____

4. How does someone look when following directions? ______________

   ____

5. Why is it important to follow directions? ______________________

   ____

6. Did you enjoy this lesson? ______________________________

7. What did you not like about this lesson? ______________________

   ____

FOLLOWING DIRECTIONS
TEACHER SURVEY

Name ______________________________ Date: ______________

1. Do you think the *Following Directions* lesson was helpful to your students? ☐ YES ☐ NO
2. Do you think the lesson was age appropriate? ☐ YES ☐ NO
3. Were there any changes you would recommend to improve the lesson? ☐ YES ☐ NO
4. Comments: ______________________________

____

____

____

Thank you for taking the time to answer these questions!
Once you are finished, please put this survey in my mailbox. As always, let me know if there are any other topics you would like me to teach a classroom lesson on.

FOLLOWING DIRECTIONS
TEACHER SURVEY

Name ______________________________ Date: ______________

1. Do you think the *Following Directions* lesson was helpful to your students? ☐ YES ☐ NO
2. Do you think the lesson was age appropriate? ☐ YES ☐ NO
3. Were there any changes you would recommend to improve the lesson? ☐ YES ☐ NO
4. Comments: ______________________________

____

____

____

Thank you for taking the time to answer these questions!
Once you are finished, please put this survey in my mailbox. As always, let me know if there are any other topics you would like me to teach a classroom lesson on.

FOLLOWING DIRECTIONS

Stop everything else you are doing

Eyes on speaker

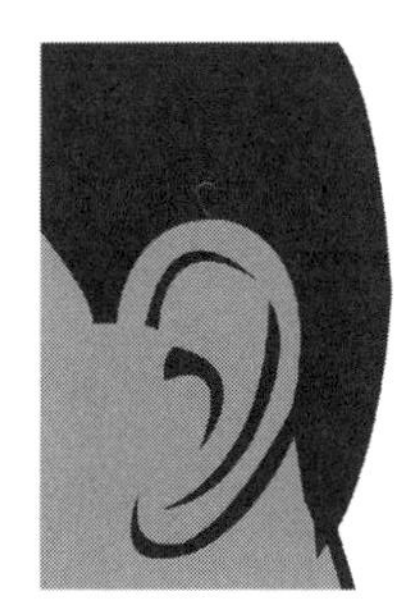

Listen

Slowly read ALL directions

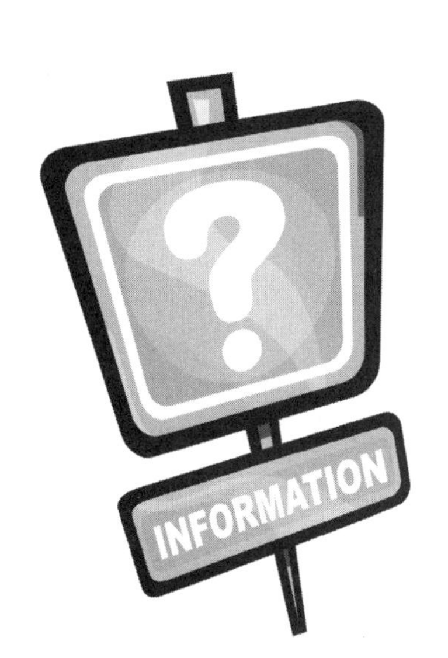

Ask questions if you do not understand

POSITIVE T-SHIRT

PROBLEM-SOLVING

GROUP NUMBER ______ PROBLEM NUMBER ______

Identify the problem situation (three or four sentences).

____
____
____
____
____

What is the problem?

____
____
____
____

How does the person in the situation feel? (List at least three feeling words.)

____
____
____
____

What could he/she or they do (choice) **and what might happen** (consequence)**?**

CHOICE	CONSEQUENCE
____________________	____________________
____________________	____________________
____________________	____________________
____________________	____________________

What does your group think is the best choice and why?

____
____
____
____

1
2
3
STRIKES
YOU'RE OUT!

CLASSROOM GUIDANCE STUDENT EVALUATION

GRADE: ______ UNIT: ____________________________

Objectives:

____

____

What did you like about the lessons?

____

____

What didn't you like about the lessons?

____

____

What did you learn from the lessons (main ideas)?

____

____

Would you recommend these lessons to other students your age?

☐ Yes
☐ No

Rate the value of the lessons to you (check one).

☐ Excellent
☐ Good
☐ Average
☐ Below Average

Please write any further comments you have about the lessons:

____

____

TEACHER EVALUATION

AND FOLLOW-UP OF CLASSROOM GUIDANCE UNIT

GRADE: _______ UNIT:_______________________________

Objectives:

____

____

____

____

How have you followed-up on the lessons?

____

____

____

____

To what extent have you observed your students apply skills or information taught during the unit? (please check your choice)

- ☐ Almost all have used them
- ☐ Most have used them
- ☐ A few have used them
- ☐ Not used at all

What did you like about the lessons?

____

____

____

What changes would you recommend?

____

____

Please feel free to make any additional comments you wish:

____

____

____

____

____

TALK IT OUT

The *Talk It Out* worksheet (see page 132) is given to students to assist them in conflict resolution. At the beginning of the school year, the counselor should have classroom guidance lessons in all classrooms focusing on the *Talk It Out* steps. Students are told they will use these steps whenever they have a problem with someone.

Teachers may also want to set up a *Talk It Out* corner in their classrooms. Then whenever students are in need of conflict resolution, teachers can give them the worksheet and direct them to the corner.

TALK IT OUT

Names of students involved:

____________________ ____________________

____________________ ____________________

____________________ ____________________

STUDENTS COMPLETE ALL STEPS

❶ **Stop**

❷ **Cool Off**

❸ **Take Turns Talking**

The Person Holding The Craft Stick Gets To Talk

❹ **Brainstorm Solutions**

❺ **Choose The Idea You Like Best.**

Signatures:

____________________ ____________________

____________________ ____________________

____________________ ____________________

CHAPTER 7

CAREER EDUCATION

What is career education?

Career education is an evolutionary process of developing competencies, skills, attitudes, and behaviors which will lead to future success in the world of work. It might better be termed career development.

The basis of a successful career for anyone is an individual who believes in himself/herself, and has the skills, attitudes, and experiences necessary for success.

Career education is an umbrella term for a process which includes:

- Awareness in the elementary school years.
- Exploration in the middle school years.
- Preparation in the secondary school years.

The goal of career education in the school is the development of students who can make informed career decisions.

Career education pervades life and school. As such, it works best when its concepts and approaches are infused into the regular academic curriculum.

Are the elementary school counselors alone responsible for career education in their schools?

The popular perception among teachers is that career education is an "add-on" to what they teach, but the reality is quite the opposite.

- Career education is, simply put, a different approach to teaching academic content.
- For example, a third grade teacher asks students to pick 10 spelling words. They are to define and use each one in a sentence that relates to a type of work or career. The academic outcome is the same, but the approach is different.
- Teachers can use *Teachers, Ask Students To Keep Their Eyes Open* (see page 138).

Are most elementary school counselors already doing career education?

Yes. Elementary school counselors are already doing career education because they are teaching decision-making, communication skills, and fostering self-esteem in many ways.

In fact, almost everything elementary counselors do is career education since employers want employees who have:

- Academic skills.
- Social and communication skills.
- Problem-solving skills.
- Positive self-images.

What are some other specific things counselors can do for career education?

In addition to those previously mentioned, there are other things that can be done:

- Establish peer helper programs (see page 157). Students help others and learn leadership skills.
- Organize career awareness months, weeks, or days.
- Organize career cluster days.
  - For example, people who work in law enforcement occupations visit the school the same day.
- Set up brown bag lunch days and invite community leaders to have lunch with a group of students and answer their questions about their jobs.
- Establish a career center with materials and activities in the library.

From the above list, the one that is the most work (but also most rewarding) is the career month or week, culminating in a Career Day.

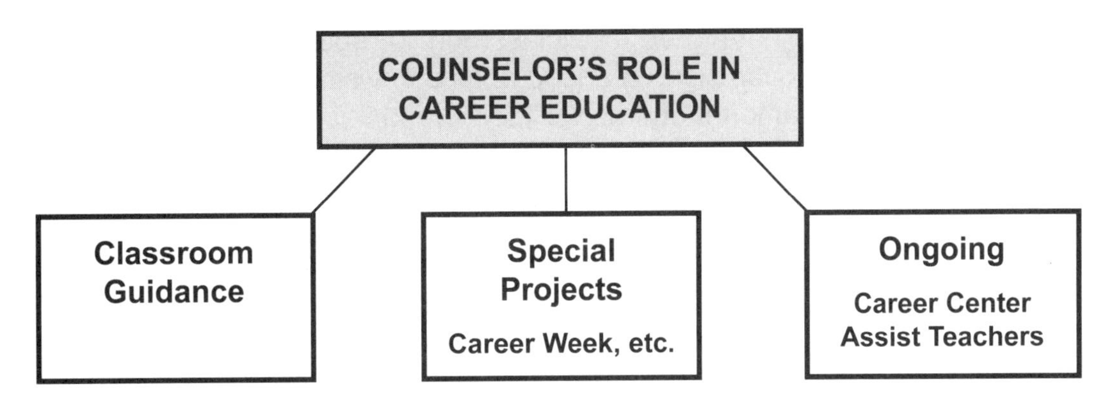

How is a Career Week or Career Day organized?

All schools are different, so the counselor should design a Career Day or Career Week that is appropriate for his/her unique school situation.

- A visit to a local vocational technical center can be helpful in deciding what careers to feature.

A good time to hold a Career Day or Career Week would be:

- In November (National Career Month).
- In February (near or during National School Counselor Week).
- Late in the year as a culminating activity.

A *Career Day* flyer (see page 139) can be used to promote the event.

How is a Career Day set up?

It is important to remember that this is a public relations opportunity for your school and the better organized the day is, the more successful it will be. The more successful it is, the better it will be viewed by everyone involved.

Choose speakers who represent a variety of occupations. Use the parents of your students whenever possible.

Prior to the actual Career Day, send a letter (see page 140) to your speakers outlining what is expected of them.

There are many ways to make the speakers available for the students. For example:

- Speakers can setup in the cafeteria or auditorium and students may pass through with their class or group. This method is recommended for grades kindergarten through second, but is also applicable for grades three through six.
- Speakers can be assigned to a classroom or space, and students in grades three through six can sign-up ahead of time to visit speakers. The speakers are given a certain amount of time for their presentations. When the allotted time has elapsed, the students move to their next choice.

Some ways to make your Career Day more successful are:

- Send *Career Awareness Speaker—Helpful Hints* (see page 141) to each speaker prior to Career Day.
- Have peer helpers and student leaders meet the scheduled community speakers and interview them in the library or media center before the program begins. Use the *Discovering The Facts* interview sheet (see page 142).
- Have refreshments available before or after the program for the speakers.
- Have students assigned to escort the speakers to their stations.
- Take photos during the session(s).
- Have the speakers return to the library after the program to process their experiences. This is important as it will give you feedback about the success of the program. The speakers will also enjoy the opportunity to talk about their role in the Career Day.

Some suggestions for follow-up are:

- Have the students in grades two through six write thank you letters to the speakers.
- Send any photos, essays, and drawings that are appropriate to their career to each speaker.
- Send a thank you letter or certificate of appreciation to each staff member for his/her support.

What are some suggested activities for a Career Week?

A Dress-Up Day when teachers wear different work uniforms or leisure activity clothes. Remember the leisure business is big business and should not be overlooked.

A Parents Career Day Lunch when parents come to school dressed in their work uniforms or clothes and share information about their careers at lunch.

An I Would Like To Be Day when students come to school dressed as a career person they would like to be.

Students can interview their parents. For this, use the *Discovering the Facts* interview sheet (see page 142). The finished interviews can be posted on a bulletin board. Names of the interviewers and interviewees can be read over the public address system.

Students in grades three through six can write essays and make drawings related to either:

- What they would like to be.
- A scheduled speaker for Career Day.

What are some important points to remember about career education?

Career education is not an "add-on." It is a different way of approaching instruction.

Career education is most effective when it is part of the regular academic curriculum.

The counselor's role is one of implementing a developmental guidance program and coordinating specific career education activities.

Outstanding resources for career education at any level are the guidelines and training packets developed by the National Occupational Information Coordinating Committee (NOICC), 2100 M Street NW, Suite 156, Washington, D.C. 20037, in the United States Department of Education.

Summary:

Career education is an umbrella term for a process spanning one's lifetime. The target of the elementary school counseling program is self-esteem, which is also the cornerstone of career education in the elementary school.

Career education is most effective when it is part of the regular school curriculum.

A Career Week or Career Day is an important activity to help students gain career awareness.

TEACHERS, ASK STUDENTS TO

Many classroom experiences—books, videos, filmstrips, and field trips—can be career awareness opportunities.

The following questions can be used to help students become aware of careers mentioned in regular classroom activities.

1. Did you see or read about anyone working?
2. What were the workers doing?
3. What are the workers called?
4. Were the workers working indoors or outside?
5. Were the workers part-time or full-time employees?
6. Did the workers work alone or with other people?
7. What kind of equipment, machines, and tools were used by the people working? What were they used for?
8. Which person would you like to help for a day?
9. Which job requires the most training or experience?
10. What are the advantages and disadvantages of the jobs you saw or read about?
11. What skills do the workers that you saw or read about need?
12. What skills are you learning in school today that would help you be successful on the jobs you read about or observed?
13. Do you think the jobs you observed or read about will be eliminated any time soon? Why or why not?
14. How do you think the jobs you observed or read about will change over the next 50 years?

CAREER DAY

Listen to:

an engineer
a fashion designer
a judge
a referee
a doctor
an office manager
a line worker
a scientist

and more people ...

tell about their jobs and answer your questions.

When ______________________________

Where ______________________________

Time ______________________________

Dear________________________________,

We are so pleased you have accepted our invitation to talk with our students on Career Day. Thank you for agreeing to participate.

Your unselfish sharing of your experience and accomplishments will help give students a realistic picture of what it takes to be successful in the world of work.

Remember to keep your vocabulary, as much as possible, at a level of understanding for 8-12 year olds. You will be speaking to three mixed-age groups. Each presentation will last 25 minutes. Please also allow time in this 25 minutes for questions and answers.

Plan to cover the training requirements of your occupation, satisfactions and frustrations of your job, expected salary and benefits, etc.

If appropriate, please wear the characteristic uniform of your job, and bring any props or equipment that are used when performing your job. For example; tennis racket for a tennis pro, easel and paint for an artist, etc.

If you have any audio visual (AV) needs, please let us know as soon as possible.

Once again, we are really looking forward to seeing you on ________________ at __________________ .

If you have any questions, please call me at (_______)________________.

Sincerely yours,

____
SCHOOL COUNSELOR

Enclosure: Map of school location

CAREER AWARENESS SPEAKER—HELPFUL HINTS

GETTING TO KNOW THEM

The students will be wearing name tags. Recognizing the students by name will give you an opportunity to gain their attention and interest more readily.

MOTIVATION

Young students are motivated by visual stimuli. Pictures, tools, equipment, and/or products associated with your work role are helpful props to bring with you. You will get a better response if the students can do something, rather than just listen.

TIME

The length of your presentation should be governed by the age of the audience. Plan for approximately 15 minutes for kindergarten, first, and second graders and 20 minutes for third, fourth, and fifth graders. Presentations that do not include visual aids or "hands-on activities" should be shorter. If props are to be passed around, you need to allow time for this. Giving out new information while individual examination of materials is going on is counterproductive.

QUESTION AND ANSWER PERIOD

Following your presentation, please allow about 10 minutes for the students to ask questions. Repeat the question prior to answering it. Knowing when to cut off discussion when the situation warrants it is a key point to remember.

RELEVANCE TO STUDENTS' CURRICULUM

It is important to help students see the connection between what one does at work and what they do in school. The connection may be in a particular subject such as math. The connection may be in an attitude toward work. Students need to recognize work as a meaningful experience that benefits society. All work has dignity, and the person doing his/her job successfully makes for a better society. The connection may be in a work skill such as punctuality. It is important to help students see that what they are learning presently in school can be of use to them later on in life.

EVERYTHING YOU EVER WANTED TO TELL STUDENTS ABOUT YOUR OCCUPATION

ELEMENTARY LEVEL:

What is your job called? What kind of work do you do?
What are the duties that you have to perform on your job?
Do you wear special clothing on the job?
What tools and equipment are necessary on the job?
What are your working conditions?
Is your work dangerous?
What made you decide upon your occupation?
Does your job require physical strength?
What part of your work do you enjoy most? Why?
What part do you enjoy least? Why?
Do you depend upon other people in order to do your job?
Do other people depend on you?
How does society benefit from your career?
How can students who are interested in your work learn more about it?
What kind of personality does one need to do your job successfully?
What type of training does one need to do your job?

DISCOVERING THE FACTS

"My name is ____________________________________.

May I ask you some questions about your job?"

1. What is your job title? ______________________________
2. What skills do you need to do your job? ______________________________
3. What is your "typical" workday like? ______________________________
4. What special training, college, and/or experience did you need for your job? ________________
5. Do you wear any special clothing? (If yes, please explain.) ____________________
6. What special equipment do you need? ______________________________
7. What do you like about your job? ______________________________
8. What do you dislike about your job? ______________________________
9. Do you get a salary or commission? ______________________________
10. If you work for commission, how does that work? ______________________________
11. What other benefits do you get besides salary? ______________________________
12. What other kinds of jobs could you have with your interests, experiences, and training?
13. When you were my age, what did you want to be? ______________________________

Remember to say "Thank You."

CHAPTER 8

COORDINATIING A COMPREHENSIVE PROGRAM

Who is responsible for the guidance and counseling program in your school?

Everyone.

Wait a minute! How can that be?

It's true that everyone is not a counselor, but everyone has a role. Without the cooperation of everyone in the school, the guidance and counseling program will not be effective.

What is the counselor's role?

The counselor's role is to coordinate direct and indirect services in order to help students learn as much as possible.

Put another way, the counselor implements both direct and indirect services, and coordinates everyone's efforts.

In Chapter 1 it was said that a balanced program had a balanced amount of time spent as follows:

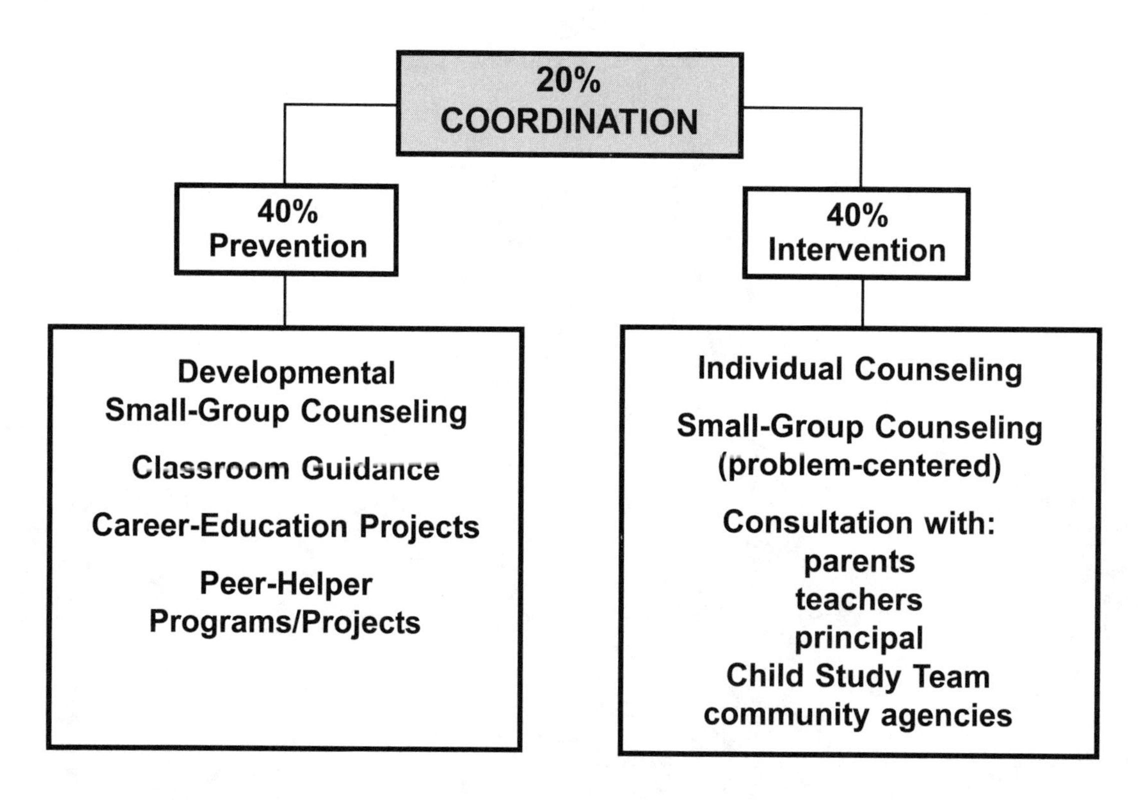

What happens if counselors spend more than 20% of their time coordinating indirect services and/or services not logically related to their program?

If this happens, the program is neither comprehensive nor balanced.

Counselors are trained to deliver services that make a direct impact on others, not to take every job that no one wants to do or has time to do. Counselors must know their role, fight for their role, tell and sell their role.

For an example of a balanced program see the *Elementary School Counseling Comprehensive Program* chart, see page 152.

What are some activities that a school counselor could logically coordinate and support?

The school counselor can:

- Coordinate multiple interventions for individual students.
- Set a schedule and stick to it.
- Have a plan in whatever you do.
- Tell about and sell your program.
- Actively participate in your school's standardized testing.
- Establish peer-helper programs.
- Keep case notes for all individuals and groups.
- Participate in staff development.
- Participate in parent education.
- Conduct career-education projects.
- Log your activities and time spent.
- Coordinate other appropriate school-wide projects and programs.
  - Testing
  - Fund-raising
  - School supplies and other donations
  - School-wide guidance programs
- Participate on Child Study and Special-Education Committees.

What is meant by coordination of multiple interventions?

This takes place when a student is involved with adults other than the counselor.

- For example, John (a third grader) might be involved with both the school and an outside agency, as follows:
  - The school counselor works with John with individual and small-group counseling.
  - The school counselor is working with John's parent(s) and teacher.
  - The school counselor is consulting with John's agency counselor (with parental permission).
  - The school counselor shares with appropriate personnel what has been done at school with the Child Study Team.
- In this role, it is imperative that the school counselor knows what community resources are available and makes use of the school social worker (if one is available) for follow-up outside of school with John and his parent(s).

Why is it important to have a plan and schedule your time?

There is always too much to do and too little time to do it all. Scheduling your time is like using a road map on a trip; you might get where you're going without one, but you almost surely will also take unwanted detours and waste time as well.

Is it important to share your yearly and weekly schedule with your principal?

Yes, definitely, because:

- It shows foresight and a professional approach on your part.
- It will help the principal to think twice before asking you to do a non-related function, such as covering a class. With a schedule, you can easily state the detrimental effect of violating it because it will mean cancelling groups, classroom guidance, etc.
- Without a schedule, you will have your time filled with ever-increasing unrelated jobs that others could do but don't want to do or don't have time to do.

What is a professional approach to scheduling your time?

The needs of students should always determine how you spend most of your time. For more information on program development see Chapter 9.

For examples, see *Yearly Guidance Schedule* (see pages 153-155) and *Counselor's Weekly Schedule* (see page 156).

What are some guidelines to follow when developing a weekly schedule?

The weekly schedule is not a master schedule but a fluid "road map" which is somewhat, but not completely, flexible due to crises or changing student needs.

Flexible time must be built into your schedule. However, since teachers and administrators may not understand the concept of scheduling, what they see is essentially "free time." It is recommended that flexible time be called consulting or coordinating time. This is what you're really doing anyway, whether it is calling parents, planning groups and lessons, following through on Child Study Team referrals, etc.

Ongoing time commitments should be blocked-off as appropriate, e.g., a Child Study Team that meets once per week.

Schedule classroom guidance on a monthly basis, such as one grade level per month for four to six lessons. It is important to remember that classroom guidance lessons are not "dog and pony shows." They are planned to meet specific objectives and infused into the regular academic curriculum as much as possible. For more information on classroom guidance see Chapter 6.

Schedule other group guidance on an "as-needed" basis, such as latchkey concerns, transition to middle school, career awareness, etc.

Remember the purpose of a schedule is to protect time to do your job, not everyone else's job.

What is telling and selling your program?

Telling and selling your program is letting as many people as possible know about your program and why it is important to the school. Your success depends a great deal on your image as a friendly, skilled adult who can help solve problems. Therefore you must make sure, as much as possible, that what you do is visible to the public. For ideas to help you tell and sell your program see Chapter 10.

What is the counselor's role in the school's standardized testing program?

Ideally, the school counselor's role should be limited to test interpretation as a service for parents and teachers. However, the reality of school climates today with an emphasis on accountability through standardized test scores, is one that often involves counselors in the coordination of standardized testing programs. As a member of a school's leadership team, the counselor should be ready to assume the coordination and implementation of a school-wide standardized testing program. When this role is assumed, counselors should remember the following activities before, during, and after testing:

BEFORE	DURING	AFTER
Create a school-wide testing calendar to distribute to faculty and parents.	Organize all testing materials for storage and distribution to teachers.	Collect and account for all testing materials.
Order any incentives you plan to use as testing motivators (pencils, ribbons).	Maintain security of all materials.	Organize and schedule all make-up testing sessions.
Attend any available training and read all related materials.	Insure that all standard procedures are followed.	Follow all guidelines for returning and storing materials.
Conduct staff development on testing procedures.	Continue incentives and motivators for students during testing period.	Analyze and interpret results for faculty and parents.
Conduct testing preparation lessons/small-group guidance for students on test taking and handling test anxiety.		
Organize motivational activities for students (poster contests, pep rallies).		
Provide information and suggestions for parents to help students be better prepared for the testing situation.		

Why is it important to keep counseling case notes?

This is a logical thing to do. It is the one way for the counselor to be sure that an accurate record is kept of the students. The counselor must take time to write notes. However, how you do it is up to you. For a suggested intake forms, see Chapter 3, pages 37-39.

If you share your counseling case notes with anyone, not only is that a breach of confidentiality, they also become "educational records" and must be kept in the student's file. Case notes are subject to court subpoena.

Is a peer facilitator program a valuable use of a counselor time?

Answer these questions:

- Do kids listen to other kids?
- Do kids pattern themselves or make role models of other kids?
- Is peer tutoring effective?
- Does having a friendly student show a new student around the school make a difference?
- Can children as young as fourth graders learn and use communication skills?
- Does a peer facilitator program result in increased self-esteem in the helpers?

The answer to all of the above questions is "yes," and there are more benefits than those listed. Coordination of a peer facilitator program is definitely a valuable use of a counselor's time.

The detailed mechanics of initiating a peer facilitator program are not covered in this book, however there are many published books to guide you.

For a description of a Peer Facilitation Program see the sample flyer on page 157. Also included is a sample of a *Parent Response Questionnaire* (see page 158) which is sent home to parents whose children have been in the peer facilitator program.

A last comment about peer facilitator programs is that in the midst of a long day full of problems, it can be wonderful to work with students who want to help others and are growing in self-confidence themselves.

What is the counselor's role in character education?

Character education has become a very popular term in schools and many state legislatures have mandated a character-education curriculum. Character education is the inclusion of values-based activities across the curriculum. The counselor can work with faculty to coordinate school-wide events to create a climate based on values.

Suggested activities:

- Monthly character-education themes such as courage, fairness, forgiveness, honesty, kindness, respect, patience, responsibility, gratitude, and loyalty supported by a book list on the topic and discussions about historical figures who demonstrated the character trait.
- Reinforce teacher morale with motivating notices. (see pages 159-160)
- Display seasonal bulletin boards (see page 161)
- Enforce a zero-tolerance policy for bullying.
- Offer small-group counseling for bullies and victims of bullying.
- School-wide recognition for citizenship as well as academics.
- Plan school-wide guidance programs (see page 162)

Why do monitorial duties (hall, lunch, bus, etc.) conflict with the counselor's role?

In many schools, counselors are assigned monitorial duties the same as teachers. If this is the school's policy, it may be best to "grin and bear it."

If it is possible to negotiate duties with your principal, stress your need for flexibility as well as your image as a "friendly adult" to students. Explain that your image may suffer if you have to discipline students.

However, teachers also dislike duties and, when the counselor is exempt from them, they may feel you are being given special privileges. This can hurt your rapport with the teachers. In order to satisfy everyone, a compromise might be in order. Offer to take bus duty so you can greet and briefly talk with students at the buses, or offer to take a duty for a teacher once in a while.

How can coordinating anything out of an "I need to be needed" or guilt mentality be avoided?

Know your role in a developmental program.

Let the results of your efforts speak for themselves.

Remember you are not a "knight on a white horse" who can handle it all. If you believe this, you're setting yourself up to fail.

Learn to "just say no" if a job or assignment is not appropriate or logical.

What is the most important month of the year to an elementary counselor?

The most important month is August, unless you are in a year-round school district, because school has not begun and the principal's and teachers' perceptions and expectations for the new year are at a positive level.

A preschool meeting with the principal is beneficial because:

- The new school year has not begun, making this the best time to present your ideas and changes in your program or role.
- You can present new ideas based, in part, on feedback data from teachers, parents, and students gained from the end of last school year. Remember, you are on sound professional ground if your suggested changes are backed-up by data.
- Once the school year starts, the principal is less likely to change anything.

Contacting teachers before school begins is beneficial because:

- Last June's burnout has mellowed over the summer and teacher outlooks are more positive.
- School has not yet started and it is a good time to share new ideas and procedures at a preschool meeting or a skill-building workshop facilitated by the counselor.

Preschool days for teachers are also an ideal time to briefly review the "what's," "why's," and especially the "why-not's," of your program.

- If time allows, this can be done at the first faculty meeting which is usually held before school opens. If not, meet with the teachers at another time early in the school year, send out a flyer, or talk individually to them about the plans and goals for your program. You can also briefly review what you can and can't do.
- If this is being done in a meeting, and time allows, have the teachers form small groups and brainstorm ways you might help students (and them) in the new year. Prioritize their suggestions.

A helpful hint to remember is that whenever you plan to do anything that affects teachers (such as a Career Day) bring it up at a faculty meeting for comment and input. This keeps teachers "in the know" and not feeling put-upon and out of the decision-making loop. Even though you may not change anything you planned to do, you asked for and considered their input. This helps keep an open relationship.

▶ Summary:

A comprehensive guidance program is balanced in two ways:

- In the services offered.
- In the amount of time spent delivering services.

If you spend time coordinating too many non-guidance functions, it will be a detriment to your program.

Scheduling your time is a must. This is the key to protecting time to do your unique job. The other key is being aware of and constantly finding ways to inform and involve others in your program.

ELEMENTARY SCHOOL COUNSELING COMPREHENSIVE PROGRAM

BALANCED PROGRAM GUIDE

GOAL: TO HELP EVERY STUDENT LEARN MORE EFFECTIVELY AND EFFICIENTLY

COUNSELING			GUIDANCE			
Personal/Social/ Problem Solving	**Academic**	**Possible Groups**	**Consulting**	**Group Guidance**	**Coordinating**	**Other**
• developmental concerns • crises • personal conflicts • communication skills • decision making • self-awareness • interpersonal relationships • parents	• information • motivation • goal setting	• self-esteem • self-discipline • communication skills • divorce/separation adjustment • children of alcoholics • peer facilitation/ leadership • developmental play • parent training/ support • Progress Club (retainees) • study skills	**Teachers** • student needs (develop strategies) • parent conferences • inservice training • test interpretation • school Guidance Advisory Committee **Parents** • student needs/ problem solving • test interpretation • parent classes/ workshops **Administrators** • problem solving • program needs • planning • test data **Specialists** • Child Study Committee member • referrals/follow-up **Community** • agencies • private services • medical	• sequential development of personal/social understandings and skills • **Grades K-1:** understanding self • **Grade 2:** understanding self and others • **Grade 3:** understanding goals, behavior, self • **Grade 4:** making personal choices, decisions • **Grades 5-6:** developing communication skills and understanding the changing self; transition to middle/jr. high school • **Grades 1-6:** study skills and test-taking • **Special needs populations**	• guidance program • liaison with school/community resources to help students • referral/follow up to help parents • inservice training for teachers/staff • orientation of students new to the school • transition of students to next school level • career awareness projects • career center • Career Week/ Career Day	• special school district-state committees • professional committees • professional training • maintain counselor log • intern supervision • public relations
Delivery Systems: • **Individual counseling** • **Small group (6-8 per group) counseling**						

Adapted from Counselors Under Construction by Mary Joe Hannaford

YEARLY GUIDANCE SCHEDULE		
MONTH	**GOALS**	**ACTIVITIES/FOCUS**
AUGUST	Understand/assess/plans for developmental guidance program	Review state guidelines/requirements Meet with building administrators to discuss school goals Meet with faculty members to get teachers' input Gather materials Order materials
	Help teachers understand and give support to the guidance program	Conduct faculty inservice—review last year and plans for new year
SEPTEMBER	Gather program-planning information	Administer student/teacher/parent/administrator needs assessment instruments
	Make the administrators and staff aware of guidance activities	Distribute a counselor schedule each week to teachers and the principal throughout the year
	Present orientation for students new to the school	First week, meet with all new students (except Kindergarten) as a group; discuss feelings; answer questions; peer facilitators/student leaders conduct orientation tour
	Meet the needs of students who were retained	On Friday of first week, meet with all retainees; discuss need for retention, feelings, and goal of improving skills and grades; follow-up with 30-minute meeting after each report card goes home, stressing each individual's progress as shown on the report card; star improved areas; call this the Progress Club.
	Introduce yourself and your program to all students	Schedule 30-minute classroom visits with each class by mid-September
	Begin weekly orientation of any student(s) who entered school during the week	Have peer facilitators/student leaders conduct a tour of school and give out a "welcome bag"
	Meet needs of individuals experiencing adjustment problems	Begin individual counseling; establish a schedule of availability; place mailbox outside door for self-referrals Begin small-group counseling—each group to meet 6-8 times for 30 minutes each: divorce/separation groups; self-concept; self-discipline; communication skills; others
	Develop career awareness	Establish a career center for students in the library
	Make staff and community aware of the counselor's role and function	Establish a guidance committee (meet once/month)
OCTOBER	Make the administration and staff aware of guidance activities	Distribute weekly counselor schedule each Monday
	Meet needs of individuals experiencing adjustment problems	Continue individual and group counseling
	School-wide, developmental program to teach all students in their classrooms sequential affective developmental concepts	Teach 4th Graders (4-6 classes) • listening skills • reflective listening • generating alternatives to deal with conflicts • predicting consequences of actions
	Develop student leaders and helpers	Solicit/screen/select peer facilitators. Begin peer facilitator training, 2 times week

YEARLY GUIDANCE SCHEDULE		
MONTH	**GOALS**	**ACTIVITIES/FOCUS**
NOVEMBER	Make the administration and staff aware of guidance activities	Distribute weekly counselor schedule each Monday
	Develop student leaders/helpers	Continue peer facilitator training
	Meet needs of individuals experiencing adjustment problems	Continue small-group and individual counseling
	Meet sequential affective developmental needs of all students	Teach 5th Graders in classrooms (4-6 classes) • "You" messages • "I" messages • accepting responsibility for consequences (weekly orientations) • learning from mistakes • seeing problems from both sides of conflict
DECEMBER	Make the administration and staff aware of guidance activities	Distribute weekly counselor schedule each Monday
	Develop student leaders/helpers	Continue peer facilitation training; reach 1/2 way point - special project: helpers lead small group discussions on friendship with a second-grade class (4 sessions) under counselor's supervision.
	Meet the needs of individuals experiencing adjustment problems	Continue small group and individual counseling
	Meet the affective developmental needs of all students	Teach 3rd Graders in classrooms (4-6 classes) • review feelings - why they are important to recognize and share with others • choices and responsibility • recognizing choices exist • problem solving • home and school responsibilities
JANUARY	Make the administration and staff aware of guidance activities	Distribute weekly counselor schedule each Monday
	Develop student leaders/helpers	Utilize helpers as "Meeters and Greeters" (weekly orientations) Utilize helpers to read to/vocabulary drill with first graders Continue formal training
	Meet the needs of individuals experiencing adjustment problems	Continue small-group and individual counseling
	Meet the affective developmental needs of all children	Teach Kindergarten classrooms (4-6 classes) • introduce feelings • sharing • working together • taking turns • care of property • responsibility
FEBRUARY	Make the administration and staff aware of guidance activities	Distribute weekly counselor schedule each Monday
	Meet the needs of individuals experiencing adjustment problems	Continue small-group and individual counseling
	Develop student leaders/helpers	Continue peer facilitation training
	Publicize counselor's role and contribution to learning	Plan and follow-through with National School Counseling Week activities

YEARLY GUIDANCE SCHEDULE		
MONTH	**GOALS**	**ACTIVITIES/FOCUS**
FEBRUARY	Meet the needs of individuals experiencing adjustment problems	Teach 1st Graders in classrooms (4-6 classes) • Review feelings and feeling words • Introduce choices as a concept • Relate feelings to choices • Relate choices to responsibilities
MARCH	Make administration and staff aware of guidance activities	Distribute weekly counselor schedule each Monday
	Develop student leaders and helpers	Conclude peer facilitator formal training Begin training for Developmental Play Program
	Meet needs of individuals experiencing adjustment problems	Continue small-group and individual counseling
	Meet affective developmental needs of all children	Teach 2nd Graders in classrooms (4-6 classes) • Review feeling words • Understanding others • Choices others make • Feeling left-out • Sharing with others; common goals • Group pressure
APRIL	Make the administration and staff aware of guidance activities	Distribute weekly counselor schedule each Monday
	Meet the needs of Kindergarten and 1st Graders who are socially, emotionally or intellectually developmentally delayed	Begin Developmental Play Program (2 times week - 20 minutes each) utilizing trained peer facilitators and identified students
	Meet the needs of individuals experiencing adjustment problems	Increase number of small groups as needed Continue individual counseling
	Present career awareness programs	Plan Career Day/Career Week
MAY	Make the administration and staff aware of guidance activities	Distribute weekly counselor schedule each Monday
	Meet the needs of Kindergarten and 1st Graders developmentally delayed	Conclude Developmental Play Program
	Meet the needs of individuals experiencing adjustment problems	Conclude small groups
	Help prepare for transition to middle/junior high school	Classroom guidance unit (2-3 classes) on preparing for middle school/junior high school
	Present career awareness programs	Infuse Language Arts and other activities related to Career Week into the regular curriculum during Career Week Third, Fourth, and Fifth Graders meet with successful community members who explain their career fields on Career Day
JUNE	Make the administration and staff aware of guidance activities	Distribute weekly counselor schedule each Monday
	Meet the needs of individuals experiencing adjustment problems	Conduct individual counseling
	Evaluate program effectiveness	Administer student/parent/teacher/administrator evaluation instruments
	Help with a successful transition to middle/junior high school	Meet with middle school counselor(s) to discuss students with special needs

COUNSELOR'S WEEKLY SCHEDULE

WEEK			TO		
TIME	MON	TUE	WED	THU	FRI
7:30-8:00	C/C	C/C	C/C	C/C	C/C
8:00-8:30	C/C	C/C	C/C	CST/EC	C/C
8:30-9:00	C/R 1	C/R 2	C/R 1	CST/EC	C/R2
9:00-9:30	C/C	C/C	C/C	CST/EC	C/C
9:30-10:00	GP1	C/C	GP1	CST/EC	GP1
10:00-10:30	C/R 3	C/R 4	C/R 3	C/C	C/R 4
10:30-11:00	C/C	C/C	C/C	C/C	C/C
11:00-11:30	GP3	GP5	GP3	GP5	GP3
11:30-12:00	GP6	GP4	GP6	GP4	GP6
12:00-12:30	LUNCH	LUNCH	LUNCH	LUNCH	LUNCH
12:30-1:00	IC	IC	IC	IC	IC
1:00-1:30	GP2	C/C	GP2	C/C	GP2
1:30-2:00	C/C	C/C	C/C	C/C	C/C
2:00-end of day	C/C	C/C	C/C	C/C	C/C

KEY TO COUNSELOR'S SCHEDULE

IC = individual counseling
GP = small-group counseling
C/R = classroom guidance
CST = Child Study Team (pre-referral interventions)
EC = Eligibility Committee (special education staffings)
C/C = consulting with teachers, parents, administrators, agencies and/or coordinating guidance services

EXPLANATION OF SCHEDULE EXAMPLE

C/R = 4 classrooms from same grade level 2x week (total of 4-6 classes for them during the month)
GP = 3 types of groups (6 in all):

GP 1, 2 and 3 are communication/self-esteem groups
GP 4 is a peer facilitator group
GP 5 and 6 are divorce adjustment groups
Groups 1, 2, 3, and 6 meet three times week
Groups 4 and 5 meet two times week

Child Study Committee or Eligibility Committee generally meets once per week; when it doesn't meet, this time is used for consulting or coordinating activities.

Note: This is not a master schedule; it will vary from week to week.

PEER FACILITATION PROGRAM

Who are peer facilitators?

Peer facilitators are special children who are leaders, positive role models, and careful listeners. Peer facilitators have the following characteristics:

- Caring
- Acceptance
- Understanding
- Trustworthiness
- Positive attitude
- Sense of humor
- Patience
- Success in school

What do peer facilitators do?

Some possible responsibilities and helping projects are to:

- Serve as peer tutors and special friends to Kindergartners.
- Help orient new students to the school.
- Lead small-group discussions.
- Provide role models for other students.
- Provide time for students who need "someone to talk with."
- Help other students learn to solve problems.
- Host visitors to the school.
- Assist the counselor.
- Assist teachers.
- Represent and/or make presentations to interested groups such as service clubs, Parent Advisory Council, etc.

What do peer facilitators learn?

Valued life skills such as:

- Communication skills.
- Planning methods to deal with problems.
- Speaking publicly.
- Teaching one-on-one.
- Listening to others intelligently without making judgments.
- Leading groups through the resolution of a problem.
- Goal-setting and follow-up.
- Learning constructive criticism.
- Empathizing with the problems of others.

How do those that interact with peer facilitators benefit?

Children who interact with peer facilitators:

- Experience trusting, caring relationships
- Observe positive peer role models
- Improve attitudes about self, others, and school
- Receive tutoring/academic help
- Learn what feelings are and how they relate to behavior
- Learn how to solve their own problems
- Learn how to set and pursue goals

PARENT RESPONSE QUESTIONNAIRE

Dear Parent:

Your child, ________________________________, has gone through extensive peer facilitator leadership training this year, learning the skills outlined on the enclosed sheet. In addition, your child has served as a role model for Kindergarten children in need of support from an older child with good communication skills. I feel he/she has contributed to making ____________________________________ School the special place it is.

I need your help! Please take a minute to provide feedback from your perspective as a parent. Please complete and return the information below as soon as possible.

Have you seen or noticed any of the skills mentioned on the attached sheet being used by your child? If yes, which ones? Please give examples.

____

____

____

____

How has your child progressed this year in terms of academics, self-confidence, ability to interact with others, etc.? (Please explain or give examples.)

____

____

____

____

Do you feel your child has benefited from the peer facilitator program? Please explain and feel free to be honest.

____

____

____

____

Sincerely yours,

PLANNING TEACHER MOTIVATORS FOR THE YEAR

THREE CHEERS...

We made it through the first week!

Because of all the "Spooktacular" things you do...

this treat's for you.

't you see how special you are to me?

Have a safe and very merry holiday!

TO GET IN SHAPE FOR THANKSGIVING, TRY THIS EXERCISE:

One-two, chew-chew-chew. Three-four, snore-snore-snore.

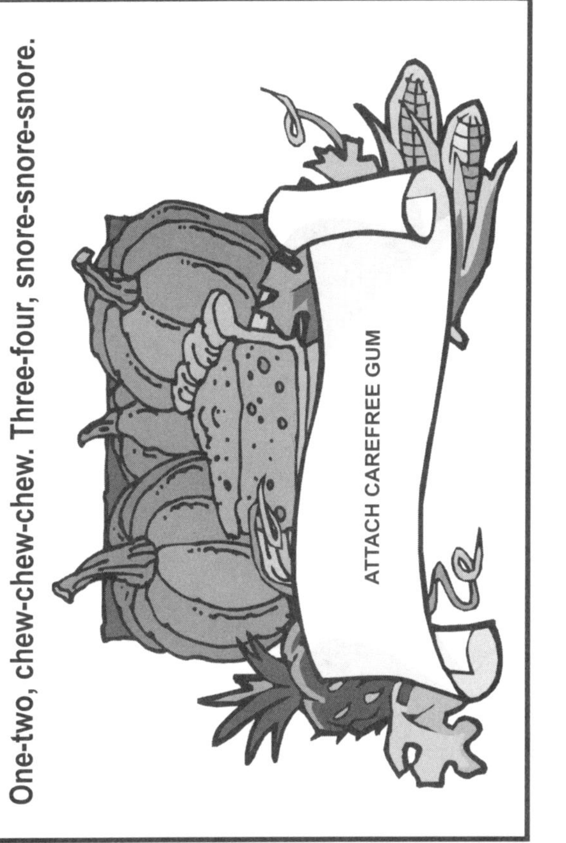

Contributed by Kathy Vienna, Jeri Weeks, Mary Pat McCartney, Sheila Murphy, Linda Trexler, Doris Clark, Nancy Lowery, Virginia Elementary School Counselors Association.

PLANNING TEACHER MOTIVATORS FOR THE YEAR

HATS OFF TO A GREAT STAFF!
Thanks for all your help and support.

STAPLE TEA BAG HERE
just for you
Oh, how happy you will be as you sip this cup of tea!

HOLD YOURSELF TOGETHER...

ATTACH COLORED PAPER CLIP

The end of the school year is near!

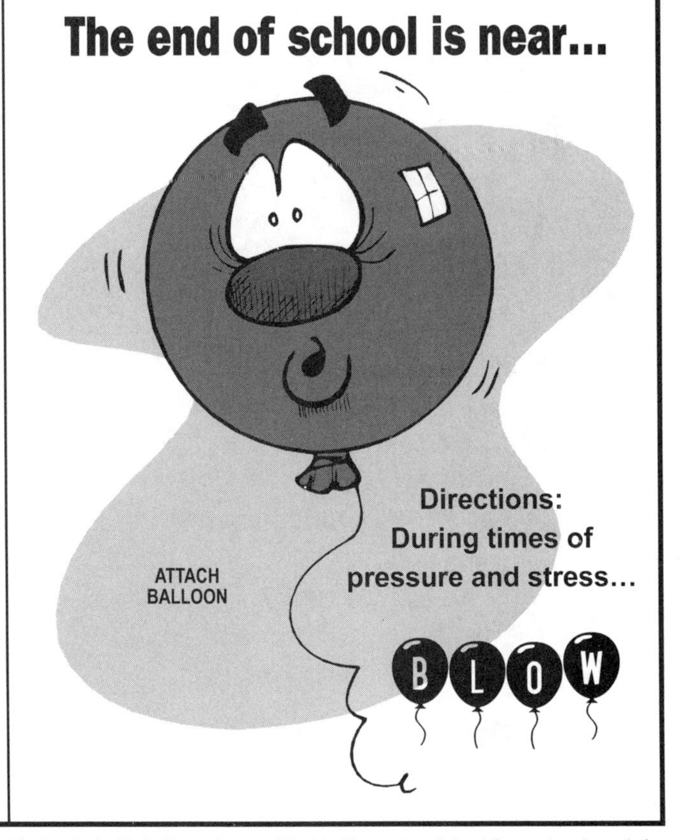
The end of school is near...
ATTACH BALLOON
Directions:
During times of pressure and stress...
BLOW

Contributed by Kathy Vienna, Jeri Weeks, Mary Pat McCartney, Sheila Murphy, Linda Trexler, Doris Clark, Nancy Lowery, Virginia Elementary School Counselors Association.

PLANNING BULLETIN BOARDS SEASON-BY-SEASON

SEPTEMBER/OCTOBER

Working Together
Students • Teachers • Parents • Counselor
KICK OFF
A GREAT YEAR!

NOVEMBER/DECEMBER

THINK POSITIVELY!

YOU'RE THE BEST!
(ADD GLITTER)

STUDENTS **SPARKLE** WITH NEW KNOWLEDGE AND CONFIDENCE

JANUARY/FEBRUARY

THROW AWAY

all the hurts,
disappointments,
grudges,
and
negative thoughts.

Focus on
the good!

MARCH/APRIL

Contributed by Jeri Weeks, Doris Clark, Nancy Lowery, Lee Johnson, Virginia Elementary School Counselors Association.

PLANNING SCHOOL-WIDE GUIDANCE PROGRAMS

SUBSTANCE ABUSE WEEK

- "Just Say No" pledge is recited over the intercom.
- "I Pledge To Remain Drug Free" Banner is signed by the students and displayed.
- "List Of Alternatives To Drug Abuse" Contest is conducted. Classes with the most creative, most feasible, and most numerous lists are awarded prizes.
- "Dress-up" Days: Be cool—wear hat and sunglasses; Don't Be Blue—wear something blue; School Pride—wear school colors.
- "Drug-Free School Zone" assembly is held.

LISTENING WEEK

- Guess That Noise: Each AM a different sound is put on announcements.
- "Good Listener" bulletin board of classroom contributions.
- Idea packet of listening games to teachers.
- Communication tips for parents in school newsletter.
- Parent workshop on "How To Talk So Kids Will Listen."
- Listening awards for students and buttons for teachers to wear.

SELF-ESTEEM WEEK

- Positive Mental Thoughts: Present each day on morning announcements (ex. "What I think of me, I'll be").
- Class Activity: Make a colorful poster on "Adjective Acronym" of students names (ex. DORIS—Delightful, Obedient, Respectful, Inquisitive, Smart).
- Journal Writings: Do a favor for someone today and write about what happened.

PRIDE IN SCHOOL WEEK

- Class Banner Contest: Each class will design a banner depicting the atmosphere and personalities of the class.
- Class Cheers: Cheers created for the school will be broadcast over AM announcements.
- Guess The Number Contest: A jar of "goodies" will be displayed and students will have the chance to guess the correct number of goodies in the jar.
- School Shield: Each student will design a shield using symbols, designs, and/or words on school pride. The shield will show: What I like best about my school. What I like best about the teachers. What I like best about being a student. Shields should be displayed in the halls.
- Writing Activity: Students write an advertisement for the school to "sell" their school.

Contributed by Mary Pat McCartney and Ginnie Ripperger, Virginia Elementary School Counselors Association.

CHAPTER 9

PROGRAM DEVELOPMENT AND EVALUATION

What are the essential elements of program development?

Plan in detail a program that meets with the school district's philosophy, the administrator's goals, and the teachers' needs. For an example of a balanced program, see *Elementary School Counseling Comprehensive Program: Balanced Program Guide* (see page 152).

When developing a program, the counselor should include:

- A needs assessment.
- Objectives and strategies to meet the objectives.
- An evaluation of the program.

For an example of a checklist, see *Program Development Checklist* (see page 172).

How important is it to measure your work?

Delivering comprehensive guidance services to students, teachers, and parents without a plan and a way to tell what works and doesn't work, is unprofessional as well as ineffective. You must make time, as a professional, not excuses.

Chapter 1 discussed "customers" for school counseling services and how their perceptions of what is or is not done as a counselor determines the support and demand for your services. Without a measurement of your work, the perceptions of your "customers" will not clearly be understood. This understanding is vital for a successful guidance program.

Why is hard data showing direct measurable results for what counselors do difficult to come by?

It is very difficult to ascertain hard data because:

- The counselor's role is to provide prevention and intervention services to help students learn and deal with interferences to learning. These types of services do not lend themselves to statistical analysis because of the many variables in human behavior.
- The counselor's role is that of an instructional support person for what occurs in the classroom. This places the counselor in a secondary position to the teacher, making it difficult to ascertain who is responsible for the student's progress.
  - For example:

    An intervention by you, the counselor, wherein you help a student deal better with frustrations and make more appropriate choices for him/herself, may result in better grades eventually—but you don't play the major part in that—the teacher and student do.

What can you as a professional counselor do to meet your "customers" needs?

A popular phrase in the business world is "get close to your customers." This also applies to counselors. They especially need to do this since they do not have total

control of their finished product. The more input you receive from your "customers" the better you will be able to serve their needs. Evaluations are a way to obtain input and feedback.

Does a program evaluation also evaluate the competency of the counselor?

No. An evaluation of program effectiveness is just that and no more. A personal evaluation of an individual counselor's skills and competencies is a personnel matter.

The results of a program evaluation should only be used to appraise the effectiveness of the program's services. It should not be part of a counselor's personal evaluation.

What is the criteria for program development?

PROGRAM DEVELOPMENT IS BASED ON THREE CRITERIA		
Needs of customers: students parents teachers	State standards and requirements used to measure the students' competencies or out-comes	School district goals and philosophy and Individual school goals and philosophy

What is the basis for a needs assessment?

The basis of a needs assessment is the identification of your "customers" concerns.

- Students
- Teachers
- Parents
- Administrators
- Staff

Does a needs assessment have to be cumbersome, highly technical, and hard to tabulate?

No. In fact, it is important to remember to keep it simple. When selecting a needs assessment, look for patterns of needs appropriate to your counselor interventions.

An instrument to measure potential topics of interest to students is a Likert Scale, which is easily converted to numbers (see page 167). With these, students rate their answers to statements from strongly agree to strongly disagree. Examples of some possible statements are:

- "I would like to know how to study better."
- "I would like to know how to act when I get angry."
- "There are things about myself that I would like to change."

Another needs assessment tool is to have the students (beginning with third grade) list five responses to questions and then rank them. After tabulating the results the counselor would then group the topics around more general needs, themes, and patterns of concerns. Examples of some possible questions are:

- "What do you want to know more about in order to get along better with others?"
- "What problems do you have in school?"
- "What are your greatest fears?"

A different tool is to list the perceived needs of the students and have them rate these using; no need, little need, some need, high need. Examples of some possible perceived needs are:

- "To have more friends in school."
- "To solve divorce-related difficulties and concerns."

Teacher, parent, and administrator needs and concerns can likewise be evaluated with a similar type of tool.

Another tool for assessing the needs of teachers, parents, and administrators is to use open-ended sentence completions. Some examples of possible questions are:

- "I am not concerned about..."
- "Students need to know more about..."

When assessing needs, also use other sources of data, such as:

- Accreditation reports.
- Dropout rates.
- Attendance reports.

Where can needs assessments be found?

Most state departments of education either have instruments for use or can recommend appropriate instruments.

The American School Counselor Association (ASCA) and your state professional association are also resources for needs assessments.

What measures (evaluates) a program's effectiveness?

Data must be collected from various sources before a program can be measured effectively. The *Data Collection Sources* chart (see page 167) shows various sources from which data can be collected.

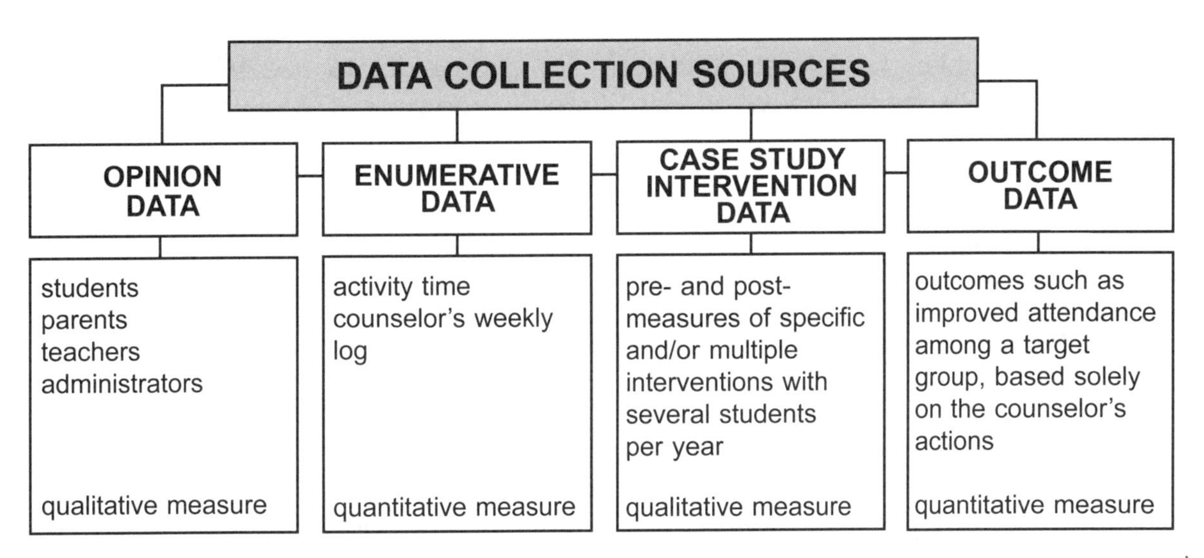

Why is opinion data important?

Although opinion data is not hard quantitative data, it is a bonafide way to get close to your "customers." Your aim, of course, is "customer" satisfaction with your services.

The "customers" for your services are the best source for feedback on your program's effectiveness. You will want to survey:

- Students (individually or in groups)
- Parents
- Teachers
- Administrators

What are some ways to collect opinion data from students?

Student opinions can be surveyed either in groups or individually.

When all the questions have been answered, tabulate the actual numbers and convert them to a percentage of total class.

When surveying students individually, it is important that the students are able to read.

A Likert Scale instrument (see below) is one way to survey students.

	STRONGLY AGREE	AGREE	NOT SURE	DISAGREE	STRONGLY DISAGREE
I like talking with my counselor					
I changed my way of doing things after talking with my counselor.					

For an example of an evaluation form for counselors to use with students, see *Elementary Guidance Evaluation For Students* (see page 173).

Randomly selected students who have seen the counselor could privately answer follow-up questions, such as:

- "Do you like to talk with your counselor?"

What are some ways to collect opinion data from parents?

Parents can be surveyed by asking questions such as:

- "Do you know if you have an elementary counselor in your school?"
- "If you have some concerns about your child's development, behavior, or progress in school, is it likely you would contact the counselor?"

Questions that require a "yes" or "no" response are easy to tabulate as are those that rate services on a five-point scale from high value to little or no value, using such questions as:

- "Is the elementary school counseling program of value to the school?"

For an example of an evaluation for parents, see *Elementary Guidance Evaluation For Parents* (see page 174).

What are some ways to collect opinion data from teachers and administrators?

One approach is to list the services provided and have them rate each from 1-4 on their frequency, importance, and effectiveness.

	FREQUENCY				IMPORTANCE				EFFECTIVENESS			
	1	2	3	4	1	2	3	4	1	2	3	4
Providing individual counseling												
Improving the school climate												

For an example of an evaluation for teachers, see *Elementary Guidance Evaluation For Teachers* (see page 175).

For an example of an evaluation for administrators, see *Elementary Guidance Evaluation For Administrators* (see page 176).

Is there an easier and quicker way to evaluate guidance programs?

Although not as thorough as the evaluation methods mentioned previously, the following questions have the advantage of non-restricting responses and can be used with any of your "customers."

- "What did you like that the counselor did this year?"
- "What would like to see dropped or changed?"
- "How can the counselor help you next school year?"

What is enumerative data?

Enumerative data is a log of what you do and how often you do it. It is strictly a quantitative—not qualitative measure.

Enumerative data can help to form positive attitudes toward the guidance program.

- Just showing your "customers" the sheer amount of services you provide can be an eye opener.
- Putting a copy of the weekly log report in each teacher's mailbox is good public relations.

The log should be simple, accessible, and easy to tabulate. For an example of a log, see *Weekly Log Chart* (see page 177).

What are the uses of the log data?

The log data can be used:

- To inform the "customers" of how the counselor's time is spent.
- By the central office staff to target staff development activities in neglected areas.
- As a time-management aid.

The keeping of a log is a professional approach akin to an attorney keeping track of billable hours.

What are some specific examples of case study and intervention data?

When constructing a case study the following should be done:

- Establish a baseline of performance frequency (see page 95).
- Identify the type(s) of intervention used.
- Measure the intervention's(s') effectiveness with pre/post or before and after ratings.
- Report data in the form of percentages, graphs, or as short narratives.

The use of pre- and post-ratings of behaviors targeted for change is recommended for several reasons:

- It is a professional approach to managing interventions.
- It can be structured to "test" certain interventions, such as a counseling group on friendship, taking turns, etc.
- It involves teachers in the process of change with the goal of improvement, thus avoiding the "fix-um" or "magic wand" mind-set teachers often have for the counselor's role.
- It enlists the teacher's support, help, and, if appropriate, a change in the teacher's way of relating to the student.

What is collaborative pooling of intervention data?

Collaborative pooling is when someone like a guidance supervisor plans and coordinates the school district's counselors in the use of specific approaches with identified populations.

- For example, after identifying common criteria in a district among third graders who are "at risk," control and experimental populations chosen at random can be exposed to the same intervention (treatment) by all the district's counselors. The results are then collected, analyzed, and reported-on.

There are many ways such collaborative studies can be organized. Local universities often are willing to be part of such research designs and can aid you in your efforts. It is important to remember to keep the study simple and easy to manage.

What are some specific examples of outcome data?

Outcome data is strictly quantitative data which is the result of specific counselor interventions. For example:

- Direct intervention with students who don't attend school regularly, but who show improvement in their attendance after small-group counseling or classroom guidance.
- Paper and pencil test results of concepts taught through classroom guidance.

What are the uses of evaluation data?

Evaluation data are used to:

- Measure progress in obtaining stated goals and objectives.
- Measure the amount of change in program areas where change took place.
- Share with your local school board, especially at budget time.
- Share with the state department of education and state counseling association.
- Share with your PTA/PTO and parents. It's easier to ask for money for resources when you can show success.
- Share with your principal. When you can show measurable results, you can build on success as you identify areas still in need of change.

The result is that you can speak to anyone about your program from a professional viewpoint, based on measurable outcomes and not on hopeful statements. For example, "96% of the parents surveyed said the guidance program was beneficial to their child(ren)" is much better than, "I think parents like the program."

What is a Guidance Advisory Committee?

A Guidance Advisory Committee is a group of people who meet with the counselor to share ideas and concerns about the guidance program in the school.

The purpose of this group would be for the counselor to receive input from the "customers" of guidance services, both to plan and evaluate, and to gain credibility for the counselor's role.

Meetings should be held monthly, with an agenda and minutes that are distributed to the teachers, administration, and the parents/PTA.

Why should a counselor take time to form a Guidance Advisory Committee?

A Guidance Advisory Committee ensures a professional approach to developing a program.

If the committee members cross disciplines, grade levels, and include parents, there will be varied input and feedback.

With a Guidance Advisory Committee, decisions are team decisions, not just the counselor's ideas.

Who should be on the Guidance Advisory Committee?

Although each school is unique, suggested membership might include:

- Two parents representing K-2nd grades and 3rd-6th grades.
- A supportive teacher to discuss ideas with or cochair the committee with you.
- Two teachers representing K-2nd grades and 3rd-6th grades.
- The principal as an advisor and nonvoting member.

What are the first tasks of the Guidance Advisory Committee?

The first tasks of a Guidance Advisory Committee are to:

- Tabulate needs assessment data.
- Develop objectives for the school guidance program.
- Develop strategies and activities to meet the objectives.
- Develop program evaluation measures.
- Correlate state standards/requirements and school district (and individual school) philosophy and goals with needs data.

In its first year, the school Guidance Advisory Committee will serve mainly to assess needs. Later on, its major contribution will be developing the school's counseling program—rather than the individual counselor's program. When this happens, the school counseling program is "our" program, not merely the counselor's program.

Summary:

Developing a comprehensive program based on the needs of your "customers" and measuring the extent of your success in meeting those needs is a professional approach. Anything less means delivering a lesser program.

PROGRAM DEVELOPMENT CHECKLIST

PLANNING

- ☐ Integrate the school district's philosophy and goals with state requirements.
- ☐ Meet with administration to gain support.
- ☐ Establish a Guidance Advisory Committee.
- ☐ Develop a timeline for program implementation.

NEEDS ASSESSMENT

- ☐ Select and administer needs assessment instruments.
- ☐ Analyze appropriate data sources, such as dropout rates, attendance patterns, accreditation reports, etc.
- ☐ Collect and summarize data.
- ☐ Prioritize needs of students.
- ☐ Assess the program's capabilities (what is being done now or has been done in the past) to meet the students' needs.
- ☐ Define changes to be made.

DESIGNING THE PROGRAM

- ☐ Write objectives to meet the students' needs (including state requirements).
- ☐ Prioritize objectives.
- ☐ Define strategies, functions, and resources (in light of who does what, when, and where).
- ☐ Design an annual and weekly schedule for the counselor.
- ☐ Design a counselor log system.

PROGRAM EVALUATION

- ☐ Select measurement techniques.
- ☐ Collect and analyze data.
- ☐ Modify program strategies based on findings.
- ☐ Report evaluation findings to "customers" and appropriate groups.

ELEMENTARY GUIDANCE EVALUATION FOR STUDENTS

Here are some questions about your counselor. We would like you to help us understand what your counselor does. Please tell us what your answer is.

	YES	NO	NOT SURE	
1				Do you know who your counselor is?
2				Do you know what he/she does at school?
3				Have you ever talked with your counselor?
4				Can you see your counselor when you want to?
5				Does the teacher send you or your classmates to see the counselor?
6				Does your counselor come to your class and talk to all of you?
7				Do you and a few other people talk to the counselor at the same time?
8				Have you learned from your counselor better ways to get along with others?
9				Sometime during this school year, has the counselor talked to you or your class about what to expect in school?
10				Has your counselor talked with you about tests you have taken?
11				Has your counselor talked with you about how well you like your studies?
12				Does your counselor talk with pupils having trouble with their studies?
13				Does your counselor talk with people who are worried or upset?
14				If you get in trouble at school, do you have to go see your counselor?
15				Has your counselor ever talked with your parents about you?
16				Has your counselor talked with you about what you might want to do when you are old enough to have a job?
17				Has your counselor given tests to your whole class?
18				Has your counselor sent you to see someone else if he/she thinks this will help?
19				Has your counselor talked with you about the reasons people behave as they do?
20				Do your counselor and teacher work together to try to help you?

ELEMENTARY GUIDANCE EVALUATION FOR PARENTS

STUDENT'S SEX __________ SCHOOL ______________________________

AGE __________________ COUNSELOR __________________________

GRADE ________________

1. Are you aware that your child's school currently provides guidance services? ☐ Yes ☐ No
2. Has the elementary counselor had contact with your child this year? ☐ Yes ☐ No
   Please comment as to whether or not this contact was helpful.
   Parent's response:
   ____
   ____
   ____
3. Have you had any contact with the elementary counselor concerning your child? ☐ Yes ☐ No
   Please comment regarding this contact. Was it helpful or beneficial?
   Parent's response:
   ____
   ____
   ____
4. How effective do you feel this program has been in helping your child meet his/her needs and in achieving suitable goals?
   Please place a check mark on the scale which best indicates your judgment of effectiveness.
   1 · · · · · 2 · · · · · 3 · · · · · 4 · · · · · 5 · · · · · 6 · · · · · 7 · · · · · 8 · · · · · 9 · · · · · 10
   NOT EFFECTIVE VERY EFFECTIVE
5. Do you have any questions, comments, or suggestions regarding the elementary guidance program or counselor?
   Parent's response:
   ____
   ____
   ____
6. Do you favor expansion or continuation of the elementary guidance program?
   Parent's response:
   ____
   ____
   ____
7. In what ways have elementary guidance services or the counselor affected your child's progress or adjustment this year?
   Parent's response:
   ____
   ____
   ____

Please return by: ____________ To: ______________________________

ELEMENTARY GUIDANCE EVALUATION FOR TEACHERS

Your response to the following questionnaire will help in understanding how people feel about the counseling and guidance services in your elementary school. Your responses to this will be completely confidential. We plan to use these responses to help us to continue to improve the counseling and guidance services. Check the box which most represents your present feelings. Be sure to put a mark on one answer for each item. There are five possible responses to each of the statements.	NOT CHARACTERISTIC OF MY PRESENT FEELINGS	SLIGHTLY CHARACTERISTIC OF MY PRESENT FEELINGS	MODERATELY CHARACTERISTIC OF MY PRESENT FEELINGS	QUITE CHARACTERISTIC OF MY PRESENT FEELINGS	HIGHLY CHARACTERISTIC OF MY PRESENT FEELINGS
The counselor was able to help children.					
Some change tended to occur after pupils had reasonable contact with the counselor.					
The counselor was interested in my feelings about my pupils.					
The counselor was able to help me understand my pupils.					
Many times the counselor was unavailable when I really needed to talk with him/her.					
Pupils seemed to enjoy talking with the counselor.					
The counselor was able to help me with my class by the things he/she said and did.					
All children should have an opportunity to talk with a counselor.					
It is necessary to have a guidance program in the elementary school.					
I use more group guidance techniques as a result of contact with my elementary school counselor.					
I am better able to help my pupils who have adjustment problems than the counselor.					
I wonder just what the counselor does.					
Pupils' classwork tends to improve after counseling contacts.					
Pupils' behavior tends to improve as a result of counseling experiences.					

ELEMENTARY GUIDANCE EVALUATION FOR ADMINISTRATORS

The items or statements listed below cover some areas in which the counselor may have made significant contributions to the pupils or to the general welfare of your school. Indicate the degree of help the program contributed to your pupils or school by placing a check in the appropriate box after each statement.

Check: Box 1—Much help has been given
Box 2—Some help has been given
Box 3—You feel that the counselor made no contributions in this area
Box 4—You do not know

	1	2	3	4
ORGANIZATION AND ADMINISTRATION				
1. The counselor has been of assistance in organizing, administering, and developing the program of guidance services.				
TEACHER INVOLVEMENT				
2. The activities of the counselor have complimented and facilitated the work of the teachers.				
3. The counselor has provided services which were beneficial to most teachers within the school.				
4. The counselor has assisted teachers in meeting the intellectual, personal, and social needs of all students.				
EMPHASIS ON THE STUDENTS				
5. The counselor has focused on and recognized good behavior as well as problems and crises.				
6. The counselor has provided services and activities of benefit to all students attending the school.				
LEARNING ENVIRONMENT				
7. The counselor has assisted in the development of wholesome attitudes towards the teacher, school, and self.				
8. The counselor has sensitized the teachers to the personal needs of students.				
9. The counselor has assisted teachers in creating an atmosphere that builds confidence, avoids threat, creates a feeling of security, and is conducive to learning.				
GENERAL AREAS OF ASSISTANCE				
10. The counselor has helped in the early identification of students with "special needs."				
11. The counselor has been of help in working with "behavior problems."				
12. The counselor has been of help in working with "gifted" students.				
13. The counselor has been of help in working with the "slow-learner."				
14. The counselor has been of help in working with "underachievers."				
15. The counselor has been of help in working with students with "reading problems."				
16. The counselor has been of help in "diagnosing learning difficulties."				
17. The counselor has helped the students in making adjustments at transitional points in their education, i.e., changing grades, changing schools, elementary to middle/jr. high school, etc.				
18. The counselor has been of help to professional staff in interpreting cumulative folder information.				
19. The counselor has been helpful in making referrals and working with "referral agencies."				
RESULTS				
20. The counselor has been instrumental in acquiring an overall higher level of achievement among students.				
21. The counselor's activities have been instrumental in decreasing the number of potential dropouts.				
22. The counselor has been of assistance in reducing absenteeism and tardiness of selected students.				
23. The counselor has been of assistance in improving work habits and study skills of students.				
24. The counselor has been instrumental in establishing a better home-school and teacher-pupil rapport.				
25. The counselor has assisted in the reduction of referrals made to the principal for disciplinary reasons.				

WEEKLY LOG CHART

NAME ____________________ WEEK OF ____________________

CODES

IC	Individual Counseling	CC	Consultation/Counselor	CR	Consultation/Resource
GC	Group Counseling	CP	Consultation/Parent	PD	Professional Duties
CG	Classroom Guidance	CT	Consultation/Teacher	PE	Parent Education
PC	Parent Counseling	CA	Consultation/Administration	CS	Child Study Team

	MONDAY	TUESDAY	WEDNESDAY	THURSDAY	FRIDAY
8:00-8:30					
8:30-9:00					
9:00-9:30					
9:30-10:00					
10:00-10:30					
10:30-11:00					
11:00-11:30					
11:30-12:00					
12:00-12:30					
12:30-1:00					
1:00-1:30					
1:30-2:00					
2:00-2:30					
2:30-3:00					
3:00-3:30					
OTHER					

CHAPTER 10

TELLING AND SELLING YOUR PROGRAM

Why should public relations be a concern?

A counseling program is a program of services. Its success depends on people using the services it provides.

In the past 30 years as elementary counseling programs began to emerge, some have fallen prey to the umbrella or shadow effect of secondary programs. This has happened because:

- Most people have at least a vague idea of what a high school counselor does, but they aren't sure as to what an elementary counselor might do.

Although many public relations ideas have already been shared in this book, here are a few more as you target your "customers" and keep them informed of the vital role elementary counselors play in student learning.

How can elementary counselors become more visible to students?

Be a part of the morning announcements each day, whether to read a poem or congratulate someone. This helps you keep in touch and lets students know you care about them.

Get the PTA/PTO to pay for birthday stickers and award these daily via the intercom.

Encourage self-response by posting a mailbox outside your room and having a supply of student referral forms (*Self-Referral Form*, page 185) and pencils nearby.

How can elementary counselors become more visible to parents?

Ask to serve on the PTA/PTO executive board. This will do these two things:

- It will help you to keep in touch with the parent leaders in the school.
- It will engender financial support for you program.

Write a monthly column in the school newsletter or send flyers home to parents citing skills, advice, and approaches parents can use. (See sample flyers, *How To Listen To Your Children* (see page 186), *How To Get Your Children To Listen To You* (see page 187), and *Developing Responsibility In Children* (see page 188).

Conduct parent support/skill-building groups.

Organize a mini-workshop parents' night, where you and your school personnel—such as the teachers, the psychologist, the social worker etc.—present 20-30 minute workshops for parents. Send out a flyer like the sample on page 181.

PARENTS REMINDER

WHAT?	PTA Meeting
WHEN?	Thursday, March 19th—7:30 p.m.
WHO?	Professionals on our staff teaching mini-workshops
WHERE?	Jefferson Elementary School
WHY?	Parents and teachers meet to work together

THEME:

WHAT PARENTS CAN DO TO HELP THEIR CHILDREN LEARN

Parents will have the choice of attending two of the following four workshops; each about 20 minutes in length.

HOMEWORK—it drives me crazy
FAMILY MEETINGS—solving problems together
SCHOOL WORK—doesn't have to be a hassle
DISCIPLINE—ways to use it effectively

IMPORTANT: Door Prizes
Six dinners for two at ____________
Two $10.00 gift booklets from ____________

Tickets for a special surprise and treat on Friday morning will be issued only to children of parents attending the PTA meeting. There will be a drawing for T-shirts, hats, frisbees, batting helmet, and school windbreaker.

YOU MUST BE PRESENT TO GET YOUR CHILD(REN) A TICKET!

How can elementary counselors become more visible to teachers?

Conduct faculty guidance inservice or staff development workshops on a regular basis, such as once a month. Do not expect all teachers to attend each workshop unless it is given during school working hours and attendance is required by the administrator. If the workshops are given after school hours, attendance should be voluntary. Some suggested workshop topics are:

- Affective teaching techniques.
- Effective methods for staff communication.
- Communication skills in the classroom.
- Positive classroom management techniques.
- Parent conferences and contacts.
- Career education.
- Test interpretation.
- Identification of special learning needs of students diagnosed as learning disabled, emotionally disturbed, ADD/ADHD, ODD, etc.

Offering and conducting staff development workshops will have three benefits. They will:

- Foster staff cohesiveness.
- Foster skill development in teachers.
- Allow teachers and principals to become more aware of your consulting skills.

Remember to conduct yourself in a professional manner in the faculty lounge. Don't be a "lounge lizard" sitting there for long periods of time. When in the faculty lounge:

- Keep the conversation positive.
- Use discretion.
- Excuse yourself politely from negative conversations.

Organize and a coordinate a Guidance Advisory Committee (see pages 170-171).

For examples of appointment and follow-through forms, see *Self-Referral Form* (see page 185) and *Follow-Up Form* (see page 189).

How can the elementary counselor be more visible to administration?

The counselor can be more visible to the principal by:

- Sharing and discussing a monthly log of activities and time spent, as well as plans for the next month. Have a schedule worked out before meeting with the principal.
- Being flexible, but sticking-up for the counselor's role whenever necessary.
- Keeping him/her informed of local, state, and national meetings you wish to attend, well in advance.

The counselor can be more visible to central office personnel and school board members by:

- Getting to know the public relations person in the central office.
- Arranging once or twice a year to make a short presentation to the school board. These presentations could include bringing in peer helpers to help explain the program or talking about the results of the counseling program at the year's end.
- Inviting staff and board members to visit your program, to attend in-service sessions, or to talk with students about your programs.

How can the elementary counselor be more visible in the community?

The counselor can be more visible in the community by:

- Making a Powerpoint or video presentation to share with civic groups.
- Arranging guidance-related window displays in local businesses.
- Inviting business and community leaders to speak at your school.

- Writing brief press releases about the counseling program. Be sure to clear all press releases with the principal and central office first. For example, you will want to publicize Career Day.
- Contacting newspaper and TV reporters and inviting them to your school. Discuss specific facts and workable ideas they would be interested in using in their newspapers or on their TV programs.
- Utilizing public service announcements on TV. They are free!
- Including relevant information about the counseling program on the school's website.

How can elementary counselors be more visible to legislators?

The counselor can be more visible to government officials by:

- Knowing the names of their local legislators and their feelings about education.
- Briefly sharing outcome data and progress reports with them.
- Getting to know the legislators' aides, as their opinions are often listened to by the legislators.

How important are the counselor's professional organizations?

Your own professional growth is essential as you gain in experience. Be a contributor as well as a consumer at local, state, and national conferences.

Two national counseling organizations that are available to join are:

- ACA—American Counseling Association
  5999 Stevenson Ave. Alexandria, VA 22304 (800) 347-6647
- ASCA—American School Counselors Association
  1101 King Street, Suite 625, Alexandria VA 22314 (800) 306-4722

Your local ASCA/ACA affiliate is especially important. It gives you:

- Professional identity.
- Networking opportunities.
- Professional growth.
- A chance to share your program with others.

Perhaps the most important question of all: Are you a manager or a leader?

- "Managers make sure things get done right; leaders make sure the right things get done." ~Warren Bennis

Summary—What makes a comprehensive program a quality program?

A comprehensive quality program has:

- Goals and objectives which are prioritized.
- The elementary counselor performing functions that are logically related to the counselor's role.
- A yearly and weekly schedule of activities that is shared with the principal and teachers.
- A counselor that is aware of his/her skill level and has a plan to seek whatever additional training is needed.
- Group guidance units that are sequentially planned and presented.
- A balance between intervention and prevention activities.
- A plan for evaluating the counseling program and a method for sharing the outcome of the evaluation with others.
- A counselor who is growing professionally.
- A counselor who knows his/her "customers." Have your teachers distribute *Speak Out* (see page 190) for the students to complete. It will enable you to decide on counseling topics.
- A counselor whose "customers" see him/her as an effective addition to the staff.
- A counselor who recognizes when change is needed and does something about it.

SELF-REFERRAL FORM

____
DATE

____ would like to see you about
NAME

____

____

I am in ____ class.
TEACHER'S NAME & ROOM #

SELF-REFERRAL FORM

____
DATE

____ would like to see you about
NAME

____

____

I am in ____ class.
TEACHER'S NAME & ROOM #

SELF-REFERRAL FORM

____
DATE

____ would like to see you about
NAME

____

____

I am in ____ class.
TEACHER'S NAME & ROOM #

HOW TO LISTEN TO YOUR CHILDREN

1 LISTEN TO THE LANGUAGE OF BEHAVIOR.
Tears, a laugh, a sullen face, a slammed door have meaning just as words do.

2 RESPOND TO VERBAL AND NONVERBAL COMMUNICATION APPROPRIATELY.
Let children realize that you accept their feelings, whatever they may be, and therefore they can verbally express them to you if desired.

3 LEARN TO RESPOND REFLECTIVELY.
Let them know what you think they are feeling at a particular moment without placing a value judgment on their feeling. For example: "You seem angry about what happened."

4 BE LESS TEACHY.
Do not get so caught up in the idea that you have to be "teaching" your children something all of the time. In doing this, you may overlook their problem of the moment.

5 REALIZE THE IMPORTANCE OF LISTENING.
This can play an important part toward enhancing your children's feelings of self-esteem and self-confidence. Listening can communicate any number of different but overlapping messages, such as: "You're a worthwhile person," and "I respect your point of view."

6 BE AN ACTIVE LISTENER.
Make a conscious and obvious effort to understand and care about what your children are saying. Listen for feelings behind their words.

7 ACCEPT EARLY LANGUAGE IMPERFECTIONS.
The English language does not always follow its own rules. Children who are constantly corrected might have difficulty being spontaneous and sharing their experiences or feelings because they fear criticism.

8 START LISTENING EARLY.
Communication between a parent and teenagers is extremely difficult if the groundwork has not been laid early. What is "important" is a relative matter and any concern children have is important to them.

9 IT IS NEVER TOO LATE.
Good communication patterns do begin early—but better communication is always possible.

HOW TO GET YOUR CHILDREN TO LISTEN TO YOU

1 **ANSWER CHILDRENS' QUESTIONS.**
Be as quick, as candid, and as forthright as possible. You can communicate any number of messages and make your children feel they are important and respected.

2 **BE AWARE OF THE IMPORTANCE OF TIMING.**
When your children ask a question, it is a sign that they are ready to listen and want your opinion. Be careful to choose an appropriate time for discussing sensitive subjects.

3 **DON'T PLAY THE PERFECT PARENT.**
It is always tempting to know all the answers. Sometimes we do know best. But sometimes we don't, and we are well advised not to pretend that we know all. Admitting that we don't know is one way of conveying that we are not perfect, that we are human, too.

4 **ALLOW FOR DISAGREEMENT.**
Sometimes parents worry that allowing children to disagree and feel free to express their side of things will undermine their respect for parents. Permitting children to disagree with us shows them that we're strong enough to be challenged and big enough to back down if necessary.

5 **ALLOW CHILDREN TO EXPRESS THEIR FEELINGS.**
Let them know we can accept their "good" feelings and their so-called "bad" feelings and still think no less of them. Telling children how they should feel will not encourage them to listen to you. In fact, it may have the opposite effect.

6 **WATCH THE USE OF LABELS.**
Your perceptions should change from month to month and year to year as your children change. Sometimes we say things in the presence of children which fix in their minds for better or for worse (more often for worse) our concept of them. Children whom we have judged or labeled will find it difficult to listen or to "hear" us for fear of being judged and labeled even more.

DEVELOPING RESPONSIBILITY IN CHILDREN

Responsibility Can Not Be "Taught," It Must Be Given.

Some Ways To Do This Are:

- Never do for children what they can do for themselves.
- Encourage children's first attempts to help you or to do things for themselves. (Remember, they are learning, so they will not be able to do the task as well as you.)
- Give children credit for trying to help out.
- Allow plenty of time to learn.
- Don't criticize or make fun of poor results. Encourage children to try again and carefully steer them toward a better way.
- When children are ready for larger responsibilities, let them handle them.
- Let children know you trust and have confidence in them.
- Praise more than you punish. Praise for effort as well as performance.
- Let your children make mistakes without feeling guilty.
- Be sure children know that their help assists the whole family.
- Admit your own mistakes when you make them.
- Never make fun of or ridicule children.
- Don't keep punishing for the same offense. Help children find better behaviors.
- Don't demand more of children than they can give.
- Remember, "Children need encouragement as plants need water and sunshine."
- Let your children make appropriate decisions for themselves.

FOLLOW-UP FORM

To: ____

I have some information regarding ______________________________

____

that I would like to share with you at your earliest convenience.

Thank you,

____
COUNSELOR

FOLLOW-UP FORM

To: ____

I have some information regarding ______________________________

____

that I would like to share with you at your earliest convenience.

Thank you,

____
COUNSELOR

FOLLOW-UP FORM

To: ____

I have some information regarding ______________________________

____

that I would like to share with you at your earliest convenience.

Thank you,

____
COUNSELOR

SPEAK OUT

Name: ______________________________ Date: ______________

1. Are you new at this school?
   ☐ Yes ☐ No

2. Do you study really hard for a test and forget all the answers on test day?
   ☐ Yes ☐ Sometimes ☐ No

3. Do you have good study skills:

A.	write down all your assignments	☐ Yes	☐ Sometimes	☐ No
B.	bring home school materials	☐ Yes	☐ Sometimes	☐ No
C.	complete your homework	☐ Yes	☐ Sometimes	☐ No
D.	study for tests	☐ Yes	☐ Sometimes	☐ No
E.	read at home	☐ Yes	☐ Sometimes	☐ No

4. Do you have an easy time making friends?
   ☐ Yes ☐ Sometimes ☐ No

5. Do your friends make you happy?
   ☐ Yes ☐ Sometimes ☐ No

6. Do other kids call you names, pick fights with you, or talk behind your back?
   ☐ Yes ☐ Sometimes ☐ No

7. Do you call other kids names, pick fights, or talk behind their backs?
   ☐ Yes ☐ Sometimes ☐ No

8. Has anyone you love died?
   ☐ Yes ☐ No

9. Do you know what the school counselor does in your school?
   ☐ Yes ☐ No

10. Do you get in trouble at school?
    ☐ Yes ☐ No

11. Do you get in trouble at home?
    ☐ Yes ☐ No

ABOUT THE AUTHOR

David Burgess holds a Master's degree in Public Administration from Western Kentucky University and a B. S. in Education from Bloomsburg University in Bloomsburg, Pennsylvania.

Dave's professional experience includes six years spent as a sixth-grade teacher and seven years as a school counselor in the public schools of Sarasota, Florida. In addition, he has had three years' experience as a school counselor in Henrico County, Virginia. In 1989, David became the elementary school counseling program supervisor for the Virginia Department of Education and an adjunct professor in the school of education for Virginia Commonwealth University. In 1995, he became a school principal in Henrico County Schools and an adjunct professor for the University of Richmond..

After receiving a commission in the U.S. Coast Guard Reserve in 1981, Dave became a certified facilitator and specialist in Total Quality Management (TQM). He retired in 1998 at the rank of Lieutenant Commander.

Dave has authored numerous articles and three books: Total Quality Counseling: A Comprehensive Manual for Elementary/Middle School Counselors; co-authored/edited Quality Leadership and the Professional School Counselor, published by the American School Counselor Association (ASCA); and The Principal's Keys: Unlocking Leadership and Learning (Successline Inc.).

Dave has consulted and given keynote speeches and workshops throughout the U.S. He has given pre-conference workshops at state counseling conferences, including "Using TQM to Improve Your School Counseling Program." He has also delivered keynote addresses entitled "Quality Leadership and the Professional School Counselor." He was a presenter at the first ASCA Advocacy Institute, and has given workshops at the ACA, ASCA and the National Association of Elementary School Principals national conventions.

Dave and his family reside in Richmond, Virginia.

INSTRUCTIONS FOR USING THE CD

The CD found inside the back cover provides ADOBE® PDF files of each lesson's reproducible pages.

For example: *Total Quality Counseling_043.pdf* is the same as page 43 in the book.

Some of the PDF files are provided in color. These pages may be printed in color or black and white. Choose the appropriate setting on your computer.

These files cannot be modified/edited.

System requirements to open PDF (.pdf) files:

Adobe Reader® 5.0 or newer (compatible with Windows 2000® or newer or Mac OS 9.0® or newer).

This CD may not be duplicated or distributed.